ZAKKA SEWING

25 JAPANESE PROJECTS FOR THE HOUSEHOLD

Therese Laskey + Chika Mori

Photography by Yoko Inoue

STC CRA⋯⋯ TABORI & CHANG | NEW YORK

Published in 2008 by Stewart, Tabori & Chang
An imprint of Harry N. Abrams, Inc.

Library of Congress Cataloging-in-Publication Data:
Laskey, Therese.
Zakka Sewing : 25 Japanese Projects for the Household /
by Therese Laskey and Chika Mori ; photography by Yoko Inoue.
p. cm. -- (STC craft)
"A Melanie Falick book."
ISBN 978-1-58479-720-3
1. Sewing--Japan. 2. Decoration and ornament--Japan. I. Mori, Chika. II. Title.
TT 705.L37 2008
646.20952--dc22
2007045889

Editor: Melanie Falick
Technical Editor: Christine Timmons
Designer: Onethread
Production Manager: Jacqueline Poirier

The text of this book was composed in Neutraface, Baskerville

Printed and bound in China
10 9 8 7 6 5 4 3 2 1

HNA
harry n. abrams, inc.
a subsidiary of La Martinière Groupe

115 West 18th Street
New York, NY 10011
www.hnabooks.com

For my friends
*Kelly, Nancy,
and Fran.*
CM

For my father,
*who opened my
eyes to the world.*
TL

Introduction

Konnichiwa!
Hello + Welcome to Zakka Sewing!

WHAT IS ZAKKA?

Zakka is a Japanese word that means "household goods" and encompasses everything from placemats and tea towels to baskets and tote bags. Zakka are functional objects, but their clever and often beautiful design is also meant to add an element of style and individuality to an environment. We think zakka are just about the cutest things we've ever seen, but the Japanese External Trade Organization has a little more formal definition: "Zakka is tableware, kitchenware, and products for the living room and dining room that are unique, ingeniously designed, high quality, artistic products possessing a sense of warmth and charm."

INSPIRATION, INFORMATION, AND IDEAS

Years ago, the phrase "Made in Japan" conjured up images of mass-produced plastic toys sold by the millions round the world. Today, "Made in Japan" brings a smile to the face of savvy crafters familiar with the beautifully designed, handmade zakka, *amigurumi* (crocheted and knitted animals), and plush toys showing up in online stores, personal blogs, and photo-sharing sites like Flickr. Thanks to the online DIY (do-it-yourself) crafting culture, the world has become a smaller place; it's easier than ever to share ideas, inspiration, and information. When one crafty blogger discovers a new series of Japanese craft books, in no time at all everyone else on the crafty Net knows about them too.

When I first found Japanese zakka books, I was awed by their beauty. They offered hundreds of great, handmade projects that I wanted to try—but all the directions were in Japanese. So, in DIY tradition, when I realized that I couldn't find the book I wanted in English, I decided to create one. I teamed up with Chika Mori who is a Japanese designer living in the U.S. and we worked together commissioning the best Japanese zakka designers. We've included all of our favorite aspects of those charming Japanese craft books—easy-to-understand directions; detailed, step-by-step how-to illustrations; and the loveliest of photos shot by Yoko Inoue, a Japanese photographer living in New York. For fun, we've added a glossary of commonly used Japanese words for crafting, a few shopping tips for buying handmade zakka and craft supplies, and a series of zakka facts throughout the projects to explain some of the cultural context and nuances of this craft vogue. For example, did you know that, in Japanese children's books, the sun is always red, not yellow? Or that Japanese women like to make fabric book covers for their paperback novels? We had fun uncovering the hows and whys of these fascinating tidbits about Japanese culture and hope you'll enjoy them as well.

ZAKKA PROJECTS

All of the 25 sewing projects in this book are authentic zakka, meaning that they were designed and made by Japanese zakka crafters living in Japan. You'll find a number of simple (and simply beautiful!) sewing projects, among them the Flower Coasters on page 78, the Sashiko Tea Towel on page 88, and the Squirrel Tea Cozy on page 142. For projects that are a little more challenging, start by looking at the Bunny Pencil Case on page 82 and the Merci Apron on page 112. And for those of you with mad sewing skills, we recommend that you jump right into the House Camera Cozy on page 60 or the Room Shoes on page 118.

Zakka Trends We've Noticed

As you flip through the book, you'll see nearly half the projects are made with linen—a beautiful fabric with a lovely hand that feels both rough and silky at the same time. In Japan, linen is widely used for making zakka and is part of a larger trend of incorporating European or French country style into home goods. We love linen, too, but wanted to include some of the *kawaii* (cute) style so popular in Japan and around the world, so we added some bunny- and bird-shaped zakka made of linen to the mix.

Using foreign words and phrases as a design element (see the Pear Purse on page 44, and the Appliqué Potholder on page 18) is another popular trend, and you'll often see this in Japanese advertising and products. Foreign words first appeared on T-shirts and clothing, and they've been carried over to zakka as well. Designers use them to give objects a modern style, and their use is thought to be cool and hip.

Modern zakka also tips its hat to *furoshiki*—the Japanese tradition of folding a piece of fabric in specific ways to elegantly or ingeniously wrap packages or gifts. A contemporary cousin of *furoshiki* is the cozy, or cover. In Japan, where there's a fondness for covering things to make them neat, there are cozies for everything! We have several cozy projects in the book, among them, the Bunko-bon Book Cover on page 28 and the Tape Measure Cozy on page 38.

Whatever you choose to make from the book, we're excited to offer you a passport to the Japanese culture of handmade zakka. Please enjoy! *Tanoshinde kudasai!*

Getting Ready:
Zakka Tools and Techniques

The projects in this book can all be made with basic sewing and crafting supplies. In a couple of cases, the materials needed may not be available locally, so we've included some resources at the back of the book (see page 151). You can also substitute your own favorite fabrics and embellishments—just be mindful of the fabric weight. For example, if a medium-weight linen is used, then you need to substitute another medium-weight fabric to produce the same look and feel of the original project.

FABRIC AND MATERIALS

Japanese zakka designers place a high value on natural, high-quality fabrics and often use linen, wool, and cotton. All these fabrics are easy to sew, and most of the projects require less than ¼ yard of fabric. Even though you won't find any polyester in these projects, if you prefer polyester or a polyester blend, both will work fine for these zakka. Note that all fabric dimensions in the projects are given with the width listed before the length.

Linen

A very popular fabric for zakka-making in Japan, linen wrinkles easily, as you probably already know. But wrinkling is not an issue when making zakka since you won't be wearing them. Linen comes in a variety of weaves and weights, and some linens are printed on one side. Unprinted linen has no right side or wrong side, but if you're working with printed linen, you'll need to use the printed side as the right side when following project directions that call for placing the fabric with right (or wrong) sides together (see page 9 for more on this).

If you don't have a fully stocked fabric store near you, you can buy linen online from one of the sources listed on page 151. Also consider recycling linen garments, curtains, or bed linens that you find at thrift stores and flea markets. And, if you can't find linen locally and don't want to order online, you can always substitute a medium-weight cotton.

Cotton

Cotton is a versatile, natural fabric that comes in a wide range of weaves and weights and endless printed designs. Several of the zakka projects call for printed cotton, and two call for solid-color, medium-weight cotton with a nice texture. For the most part, you just need a small scrap of fabric for these projects, providing a perfect opportunity to use something from your fabric stash.

Like solid-color linen, solid-color cotton has no right or wrong side. But if you're working with a printed cotton, use the printed side as the right side when project directions call for placing the fabric's right or wrong sides together (see page 9 for more on this).

Wool and Wool Felt

Woven wool fabric and wool felt are also used for zakka-making. You'll find lots of wool fabric choices in your local fabric store, but nice wool felt may be a little harder to source, so, if necessary, check the Resources on page 151. If need be, you can substitute acrylic craft felt for wool felt.

Wool felt and most wool fabrics do not have a right or wrong side to worry about when following the project directions. And since the cut edges of wool felt do not unravel, there's no need to finish the edges in any way.

Cotton Batting

Batting is used in some projects to add a little padding or dimension. It is widely available in the United States in a variety of weights and fibers, including polyester, but the Japanese generally stick with cotton batting because of their preference for natural fibers. Nonetheless, you can easily substitute a polyester batting for the zakka projects in this book and get good results.

Interfacing

Several projects call for fusible interfacing, which provides stability to a lightweight fabric. Interfacing is sold in fabric stores and comes in many varieties and weights. We recommend woven-cotton fusible interfacing because we think it drapes better than nonwoven interfacing; and for most projects in this book, a lightweight interfacing is ideal. When you buy interfacing, request the manufacturer's instructions for adhering the interfacing to the fabric (these directions vary by product).

A BASIC MATERIALS LIST

Below is a list of general supplies that will be useful to have on hand when making any of the projects in this book. Additional supplies are called for in the materials list at the start of each project.

Assortment of hand-sewing and embroidery needles

Sewing machine (although all projects can also be made by hand)

Straight pins

All-purpose thread

Fabric scissors

Seam ripper

Water-soluble, disappearing-ink fabric-marking pen

Tape measure

SEWING TECHNIQUES

Sewing zakka is easy, fun, and rewarding—and you can make most of the projects in this book in an afternoon with basic sewing skills. As you look through the photographs on these pages, you'll notice the designers' fine workmanship and meticulous attention to detail. This is hardly surprising since Japan has a long, impressive history of and reverence for art and craft, and it's a country in which many of its artisans are named official National Living Treasures.

Transferring Patterns and Motifs

Some projects call for transferring a template or pattern onto fabric, and there are several ways do this. The most direct way—provided your fabric is sheer enough—is to lay the fabric over the template and trace the pattern with a water-soluble, disappearing-ink, fabric-marking pen. (It's always a good idea to test the pen on a scrap to double-check that the ink will wash out before using it on your actual project fabric.)

A variation on this approach is to hold the fabric with the pattern underneath it up to a window and see if the design shows through enough to trace it. If it does, tape the pattern and fabric to the window, and use the disappearing-ink pen to trace the design.

Using a light box is another, more sophisticated version of the two transfer methods above. The light box itself is a simple device that's available in art-supply stores but which you can easily make at home if you're handy and so inclined. It consists of nothing more than a wooden box with a translucent glass or Plexiglas window on top and a light source underneath the glass to illuminate what's on top. To transfer a template using a light box, tape the template on top of the glass/Plexiglas window and the fabric on top of the template. Then turn on the light underneath the window to illuminate the template and fabric atop it, and trace the design onto the fabric with the disappearing-ink pen.

Finally, if you're working with a medium- or heavyweight fabric like heavy linen or wool that's not transparent enough for the methods described above, lay dressmaker's carbon paper, carbon-side down, on top of the fabric and place the template on top of the carbon paper. Then trace over the image with a fine ballpoint pen to transfer the design to the fabric. (Dressmaker's carbon paper is available in fabric-supply stores or from online sewing sources and is generally sold in packets with several colors of carbon, so you can transfer patterns or markings to fabrics of different colors. Traditionally sewers use what's called a marking wheel with the dressmaker's carbon to transfer the pattern or marking, but tracing with a fine ballpoint pen also works.)

Seams and Seam Allowances

When making a seam to join two (or more) fabrics, you'll sew the seam at a certain distance from the fabrics' aligned edges. The fabric that extends from the seam to the cut edge is referred to as the seam allowance and defines how wide the seam is (that is, a $1/2$"-wide seam is a seam with $1/2$"-wide seam allowances). The width of the seam allowance to be used throughout a project is clearly marked at the beginning of the project; and, if a project has a pattern, the pattern shows the seam lines marked as dashed stitching lines. Occasionally a project requires seams of two different widths, in which case the directions tell you how wide to make each one. To establish the seam's correct width when using a sewing machine, set the aligned fabric edges that you're joining at the indicated width to the right of the machine's needle.

Most machines have measured guides for seam lines on the metal plate under the needle. If yours doesn't, you can mark a specific seam width by placing masking tape temporarily at the correct distance to the right of the needle on the metal plate below it or by slipping a large rubber band over the machine's arm and around the bottom of the machine, positioning it at the correct distance to the right of the needle. Then just keep an eye on the aligned edges of the fabric as you sew to be sure that they stay consistently aligned with the marked guideline.

Fabrics—Right or Wrong Sides Together?

Sometimes the project directions will tell you to position the fabrics with right sides together—or with wrong sides together—for sewing. Positioning the fabric with right sides together before sewing them means to place one fabric's right side (its printed or embellished side) so that it faces the right side of the other fabric to which it's being joined. Once the fabrics are positioned this way, you'll see and work from the fabrics' wrong side. After you sew the two fabrics together, the directions will tell you to turn them right side out, and the seams will be hidden on the inside of the project.

Some fabrics, for example, a solid-color, unprinted cotton, will have no right or wrong side because both sides of the fabric are the same. In that case, either side of the fabric can become its right or wrong side, provided that you haven't embellished one side, which automatically makes that side the right side, or that you haven't cut the fabric with a pattern piece whose shape establishes one side as the right or wrong side.

To help you keep track of the right and wrong side of the fabrics as you work through a project's directions, the step-by-step illustrations note the side of the fabric you see in each drawing.

Basting a Seam

Basting is used to temporarily stitch two pieces of fabric together before sewing a permanent seam. You can baste by machine or by hand. To baste by machine, set your sewing machine to the longest stitch possible, usually 4mm (about six stitches per inch), align the fabric edges to be basted together, and stitch away. Then, after you've sewn the permanent seam, use a seam ripper to remove the basting stitches if they will show in the finished project.

To baste by hand, thread a hand-sewing needle, but don't knot it. Instead, after aligning the edges to be basted, start basting by taking a backstitch (see page 11) to anchor the thread, and then sew ¼"-long running stitches (see below) along the length that you need to baste. Instead of knotting the thread at the end of your basted stitching line, just leave a long thread tail. Once you no longer need the basting stitches, clip the backstitch and pull out the thread.

Backstitching a Seam with a Machine

Backstitching by machine (which is different than the hand-embroidery stitch called backstitching on page 11) refers to the process used to secure the beginning or end—or both—of your stitching line. To backstitch at the beginning of a stitching line, position the fabric under the needle two or three stitches ahead of where you want to start stitching. Lower the needle into the fabric, put your machine in reverse mode, and stitch several stitches in reverse until you get to your starting point. Set your machine for forward stitching, sew back over your backstitches, and continue forward.

To backstitch when you arrive at the end of your stitching line, again set your machine to sew in reverse and slowly sew several stitches over the last few stitches you made. Lift the presser foot, and pull several-inch-long thread tails from both the top and bobbin threads before you clip the threads to release the fabric from the machine. Then, if you're sewing on the right side of the fabric, thread the top thread on the right side into a hand-sewing needle, insert the needle into the fabric's right side, bring it out on the fabric's wrong side, and knot the thread with the bobbin thread on the fabric's wrong side (then do the same with the thread tail at the beginning of your stitching line). If you are sewing with the two fabrics' right sides together (that is, you're working from the fabric's wrong side), just clip the thread tails. When you turn the work right side out, the remaining thread tails will be hidden inside the work.

Clipping and Notching Curved Seams

Whenever an edge is curved, whether inward or outward, it's helpful to trim the curve so that the seam allowance lies flat inside the piece: If an inward curve is sharp, there's very little room for the bulk of the seam allowance, which must fold on itself to fit into this tight space. To flatten the seam allowance on an inward curve, clip it at several points (see *Drawing A*), being careful not to clip into the seam itself. Now the seam allowance can "contract" and lie flat inside the curve.

A sharp outward curve may pull the seam allowance tight and cause it to buckle as it tries to stretch over the full span of the curve. To ease the tension, notch the fabric at several points along the curve, cutting small triangle shapes out of the seam allowance (see *Drawing B*) and, again, being careful not cut the seam itself. Notching allows the seam allowance to spread out and lie flat along the outward curve.

Pressing Seam Allowances

After permanently sewing a seam, the project directions may tell you to press the seam open. That means to press the two seam allowances in opposite directions away from the stitched seam itself, which will reduce bulk (meaning that there will be only two layers of fabric on each side of the seam rather than three layers on one side if the seam is left unpressed). If a project does not specify pressing the seam open, you can leave it unpressed, and the seam's bulk will not be an issue in constructing the project.

Finishing Seam Allowances

There are a several ways to finish the cut edges of a seam so that they will not fray. The simplest and quickest method is to trim the edge of each seam allowance with pinking shears. The zigzag cuts that pinking shears produce cut the fabric back and forth in tiny diagonal segments across its bias, which significantly reduces fraying since bias cuts don't unravel. When cutting with your pinking shears, be sure to cut near the fabric's edge, so you don't reduce the width of the seam allowances too much and weaken the seam's strength.

A Clip inward curve.

B Notch outward curve.

Another way to finish a seam's edge is to set your sewing machine for a zigzag stitch and zigzag along the raw edge of each seam allowance, "binding" the cut edge and prevent it from fraying. After zigzagging, use small scissors to trim any stray threads.

A third—and elegant—way to finish a seam is to turn and press the raw edge of each seam allowance ¼" to the wrong side and then edge-stitch (see below) each pressed fold in place. Make sure to isolate the folded edge under the needle before you begin stitching so that you won't inadvertently stitch the seam allowance to the project fabric beneath it.

Edge-Stitching and Topstitching

Edge-stitching and topstitching are closely related. They both involve straight-stitching and can be used to finish and reinforce an edge, attach an appliqué edge, or decorate a surface. The simple difference between edge-stitching and topstitching is really the distance at which the stitches are sewn from the edge.

Edge-stitching, as its name implies, is sewn very close to the folded or cut edge itself—about ¹⁄₁₆" to ⅛" from that edge. Topstitching sits more than ⅛" from the fabric's edge and could be sewn at any greater distance from the edge, from ¼" to 5" or maybe even 10" or more away. In the end, the difference between edge-stitching and topstitching is largely one of semantics since they both involve straight-stitching along, or at varying distances from, an edge, and all of the project directions in this book indicate how far from the edge to stitch.

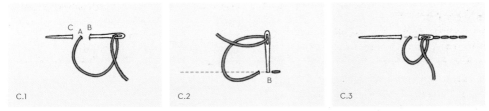

C.1   C.2   C.3

HAND STITCHES

Although the directions for all the zakka projects in this book call for machine-sewing, these pieces can also be sewn by hand. You can substitute small running stitches (page 14) for standard machine-stitching; or, if you need a stronger seam for a project like the Cross Tote Bag on page 50, whose seams will get a lot of wear and tear, you can use a backstitch. In addition to the regular construction stitching, a number of the projects are also decorated with hand embroidery. On the next few pages is a glossary of both functional and decorative hand stitches used in the projects.

For construction stitching by hand, you'll need all-purpose sewing thread (use the thread doubled in your needle) and a sharp, which is the most common type of hand-sewing needle. Sharps come in various sizes from 1 to 10 (the larger the number, the smaller the needle), and a size 7 to 9 sharp will work for most needs. To sew with decorative embroidery floss, use an embroidery or crewel needle, which has a longer eye for the floss to pass through.

Backstitch

The backstitch is a simple but very strong stitch that can be used both functionally and as a decorative embroidery stitch (for information on backstitching by machine, which is entirely different, see page 9). As a functional stitch, the backstitch can substitute for machine-stitching when a strong, hand-sewn seam is needed. When used for embroidery, this stitch generally outlines a shape. In the case of The Pear Purse (see page 44), backstitching is used to create the lettering on the front of the purse.

Work the backstitch from right to left (or from left to right if you're left-handed). Place your threaded needle under the fabric, and bring it up through the fabric at the point where you want to begin stitching (A in *Drawing C.1*). Insert the needle in back of A into B, pass it under the fabric, and bring it up and pull the thread through at C, which is one stitch length ahead of A. You've now completed one backstitch.

To make the next stitch, insert the needle just ahead of the last completed stitch, (at B in *Drawing C.2*), pass it under the fabric one stitch length ahead of A, the first stitch. Repeat this sequence, sewing your stitches consistently the same length and with the same tension, moving backward and forward to form a row of stitches in a straight or curved line, depending on what your design calls for *(Drawing C.3)*. At the end of your stitching line, pull your needle through to the wrong side of the fabric and knot off your thread.

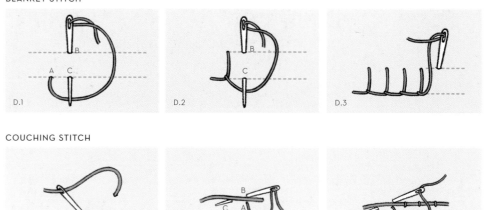

BLANKET STITCH

D.1 D.2 D.3

COUCHING STITCH

E.1 E.2 E.3

Blanket Stitch

The blanket stitch is both functional and decorative, and is often used for working an edge or for appliquéing one fabric to another.

Work the blanket stitch from left to right (or from right to left if you're left-handed) with the thread moving between two imaginary parallel lines about ¼" apart, as shown in *Drawing D.1.* Bring the threaded needle up from behind the fabric at A on the bottom line. Insert the needle at B, about ⅛" to ¼" to the side of A on the top line, and come back out at C, directly below B. Before pulling the needle all the way through, make sure the thread is under the needle.

Start the next stitch by inserting the needle on the top line, at B in *Drawing D.2,* ⅛" to ¼" to the right of the previous stitch (the same distance you used in the first stitch), and bring the needle out at C on the bottom line, with the thread under needle. Continue working the stitches across the fabric this way, keeping their height and width the same *(Drawing D.3).* To finish, take a small stitch or two into the last loop, pass the needle to the fabric's wrong side, and knot off the thread.

Couching Stitch

The couching stitch is an easy-to-sew decorative embroidery stitch that involves laying a thick thread (like embroidery floss) on the fabric and securing it with a series of stitches using another thread. The couching thread is usually finer than the thread being couched, so, if you're working with floss, separate a couple strands from a length of floss to couch with. If you want the couching stitches to be seen, use a color of floss that contrasts with the thread being couched. If you want the couching stitches to be subtle or invisible, use a matching or similar floss color.

Work the couching stitch from right to left (or from left to right if you're left-handed). Start by bringing up the thread to be couched from the fabric's wrong side and laying it in the position in which you want to couch it *(Drawing E.1).* Then bring the separate couching thread up from the wrong side of the fabric at the point where you want to start couching the first thread, shown at A in *Drawing E.2.* Use one hand to hold the thread being couched flat and in place, and the other hand to sew the couching stitches along this thread. The couching thread should be just below the line of thread you're holding in place. Insert your needle at B on the other side of the thread being couched, and exit at C, below the thread being couched and about ⅛" to the left of B. Where the thread exits the fabric at C now becomes the starting point for the next couching stitch. Continue as shown in *Drawing E.3.* When you've finished couching, pass each of the two threaded needles to the back of the work, and knot off each thread.

FISHBONE STITCH

 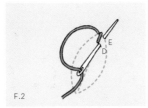  

F.1   F.2   F.3   F.4

FRENCH KNOT

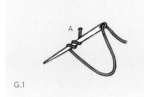  

G.1   G.2   G.3

Fishbone Stitch

The fishbone stitch is a decorative stitch used to fill a small area like a leaf or flower petal. To make a fishbone stitch to fill a leaf shape, first establish where the leaf's outline and center line will be (mark these lines with a disappearing-ink pen). Begin the stitch by bringing your needle up from the wrong side of the fabric, shown at A in *Drawing F.1*, and insert the needle a short distance away down the leaf's center line at B. Then bring your needle back up at C on the leaf's outer edge, close to A.

Insert your needle back down at D, crossing over the base of the first stitch, and bring the needle out at E, on the leaf's outer edge close to the other side of A *(Drawing F.2)*. Insert your needle at F, crossing over the base of the last stitch, and come out on the leaf's outer edge at G *(Drawing F.3)*. Repeat the steps for stitches D through G on alternating sides, crossing over the base of the last stitch, hugging the outer edge of the leaf shape, and keeping the tension of your stitches even so they'll lie flat *(Drawing F.4)*. After filling the entire shape, knot off your floss on the fabric's wrong side.

French Knot

The French knot is easy to make and, worked in several strands of embroidery floss, produces a nice, rounded knot to decorate a surface or add, for example, a center to a flower. Worked closely together, French knots produce a beautiful, textured surface.

Start a French knot by bringing the needle up from the fabric's wrong side, shown at A in *Drawing G.1*. Hold the floss tightly in one hand, and wrap it around the needle twice. Then, holding the wrapped floss tightly in place at the needle's tip, insert the needle back into the fabric very near, but not actually in, A *(Drawing G.2)* and pull the thread through to the wrong side to form the knot *(Drawing G.3)*. (If you insert the needle back into A and pull it through to the wrong side, you'll lose the French knot and have to start all over.) To make a bigger knot, wrap the floss around the needle a couple more times before inserting the needle back into the fabric or use more strands of floss in your needle. To complete the knot, knot off the floss on the fabric's wrong side.

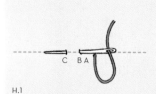

Stitches should be a little longer
than the space between them.

Gathering Stitch

A gathering stitch is functional stitch used to gather a
length or area of fabric. You can sew it either by
machine or by hand.

To sew a gathering stitch by machine, first loosen your
machine's thread-tension setting (see your machine
manual for instructions) so that the bobbin thread on the
back of the fabric will be looser than the thread on the
front. Next set the stitch length to its longest setting—
about 4mm, or six stitches to the inch—and sew two rows
of stitches, one below the other, about ⅛" to ¼" apart.
Leave thread tails a couple of inches long at the beginning
and end of each line of gathering stitches. Then, after
taking the fabric out of the machine, gently pull the
bobbin-thread tails on the back of the fabric at each end
of your stitching line to gather up the fabric to the length
needed. Spread the gathers out evenly, and secure each
end by threading the thread tails into a hand-sewing
needle and knotting the threads on the back of the fabric.

To gather by hand, start with a doubled and knotted
thread in your hand-sewing needle, and sew a row of
loose, evenly spaced, running stitches (see above) about
¼" to ⅜" long (with the stitches and spaces between
them the same length) along the length of fabric to be
gathered. Then pull the thread at the end of the row to
gather up the fabric to the length you need, and knot the
thread on the back of the fabric. Distribute the gathers
evenly before you sew the edge permanently or join it to
another cut fabric piece.

Running Stitch

The running stitch is perhaps the most basic of functional
stitches and is very easy to sew. If you want to sew the
projects in this book by hand rather than by machine,
you can stitch the seams with a running stitch, provided
those seams don't need to be strong and take a lot of
wear. If they do, use the backstitch instead on page 11.

Sew the running stitch from right to left (or left to right if
you're left-handed). Start by bringing your threaded
needle up from the wrong side of the fabric, shown at A
in *Drawing H.1,* then insert it back down through the
fabric at B. Skip a space that's equal to the length of the
stitch you've just made, and come up at C to start a new
running stitch. Continue repeating this process to create
a line of running stitches (*Drawing H.2*).

Be careful as you're sewing to keep both your stitches
and the spaces between them a consistent length,
typically ⅛" to ¼" long. Also make sure to always sew
with the same tension, so the stitches lie flat rather than
bunching up along the stitching line.

Sashiko Stitch

The sashiko stitch is a decorative variation on the running
stitch (see above). Unlike the running stitch, which calls
for making all stitches and spaces between them the
same length, the recommended stitch ratio for the
sashiko stitch is 3 to 2, meaning that the stitches should be
slightly longer than the spaces between them, as shown in
Drawing I.

SATIN STITCH

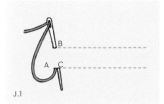 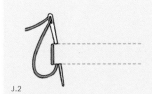 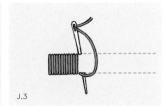

J.1   J.2   J.3

SLIPSTITCH   WHIPSTITCH

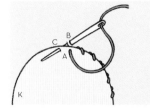 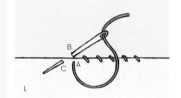

K   L

Satin Stitch

A satin stitch is a decorative embroidery stitch used to fill an area. The stitch itself is easy to do, but it may take some practice to get the fill stitches to lie flat and line up evenly. Be sure to fill in the designated area with enough satin stitches so that the fabric underneath doesn't show through. Note that, in *Drawings J.1* through *J.3,* the area being filled falls between two parallel lines. In fact, you can use a satin stitch to fill an area of any shape.

To work a satin stitch, start by bringing a threaded needle up from the back of the fabric, as shown at A in *Drawing J.1.* Then insert the needle back down in the fabric at B. Bring the needle back up at C. Start the process again, as shown in *Drawing J.2,* and continue making satin stitches to fill in the entire area *(Drawing J.3).* Then knot off the thread on the back of the work.

Slipstitch

A slipstitch is a functional stitch used to join two edges of fabric from the right side with stitches that are almost invisible. It's often used to attach an appliqué to another fabric, as in many of the projects in this book. When slipstitching, use thread that closely matches the fabric's color and a fine, small needle to help keep these stitches as invisible as possible.

Work a slipstitch from the right to the left (or left to right if you're left-handed), and start by bringing your needle up from the back of the base fabric and through the edge of the appliqué, as shown at A in *Drawing K.* Take a

tiny stitch into the base fabric directly opposite A at B. Stitch back into the appliqué's edge at C, about ¼" along the edge and catching just a couple threads with your needle. Then take a tiny stitch back into the base directly opposite your last stitch in the edge of the appliqué. Continue sewing in this way until you've finished attaching the appliqué, then knot off the thread on the wrong side of the base fabric.

Whipstitch

Like the slipstitch above, a whipstitch is a good, functional stitch for attaching an appliqué to another fabric or for joining two edges.

To attach an appliqué to another fabric (or join two edges) with whipstitches, position the appliqué, then bring the needle up from the wrong side of the fabric through the edge of the appliqué, as shown at A in *Drawing L.* Then insert the needle behind the appliqué's edge, taking a bite of the base fabric (as shown at B), and bring the needle diagonally back up through the appliqué's edge at C. Continue taking angled stitches across the edge of the appliqué and tiny bites of the base fabric beneath, keeping the angle, length, and distance between the whipstitches consistently even. Then knot off the thread on the back of the work.

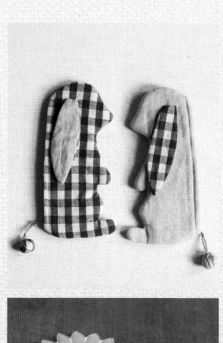

PROJECTS

appliqué
pot holder

- -

Ditch your old worn-out oven
mitts, and whip up this pot holder
to give your table presentation
flair. Add a decorative label on top
(the one shown on page 20 is the
Russian word for "lines"). Use a
printed twill tape or embroider
a phrase to fit your style.

Zakka Fact

Kitchens in Japan are quite
small, and Japanese cooks
use a stove top much more
than an oven—think stir-fry,
miso soup, and steamed
vegetables. Although this
pot holder has a layer of
cotton batting, please
remember to use it *only* for
handling stove top pots
and pans—it isn't thick
enough for removing hot
pans from the oven.

Level of Difficulty

- -

Finished Size

5" x 7¼";
doubled leather loop, 1½" long

Materials

FABRIC

Fabric A: ¼ yard of undyed muslin or cotton, cut into 2 rectangles, 5½" x 7¾" *(for pot holder's front and back)*; 1 rectangle, 1½" x 5½" *(for appliqué)*

Fabric B: Scrap of blue vegetable-print cotton, cut to 1¼" x 1½"

Fabric C: Scrap of natural-colored linen, cut to 3½" x 5¼"

Fabric D: Scrap of blue/white checked cotton, cut to 1" x 2½"

Fabric E: Scrap of small-flower-print cotton, cut to ¾" x 5¼"

TRIM

2½" length of ¾"-wide red grosgrain ribbon

Decorative label, ⅝" x 2⅝"

Off white strip of thin leather/suede, 3/16" x 3"

OTHER SUPPLIES

Scrap of flat cotton batting, 4¾" x 6⅞"

Pinking shears

All-purpose sewing thread in off white

- -

Seam Allowance

3/8"

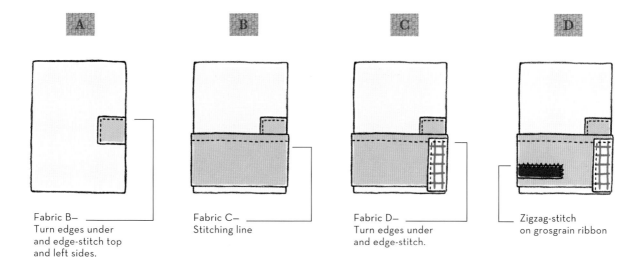

A

B

C

D

Fabric B—
Turn edges under
and edge-stitch top
and left sides.

Fabric C—
Stitching line

Fabric D—
Turn edges under
and edge-stitch.

Zigzag-stitch
on grosgrain ribbon

1. Appliqué Fabric on Pot Holder Front

Sew each fabric appliqué on the right side of the pot holder's front *(Fabric A)* by edge-stitching (see page 10) the appliqué in place. It's important to follow the appliqué order below since each fabric is layered over the previous one. Keep things simple by using an off white thread for all the edge-stitching; or, for a bolder look, try a contrasting thread color. Refer to the photograph at left and illustrations on this and the next two pages for positioning each appliqué.

Fabric B: Turn under the blue vegetable-print cotton's edge ⅛" as you edge-stitch only its top and left edges to the pot holder (the other edges will be caught by one of the other appliqués and/or by the seam you'll sew in Step 2 to join the pot holder front and back) *(Drawing A)*.

Fabric C: Pin the linen in place so that top raw edge overlaps the bottom edge of the blue vegetable-print cotton by ¼", and sew only the linen's top edge in place *(Drawing B)*. Note that you'll fray the linen's top edge by hand in Step 4.

Fabric D: Edge-stitch the blue/white checked fabric on top of the linen, turning the top and left edges under ⅛" as you sew. Make sure to position this fabric just below the top edge of the linen so that it doesn't cover the ends of the linen edge that will be frayed *(Drawing C)*.

Red Grosgrain Ribbon: Layer the ribbon on the lower left edge of the linen, and attach its top and right edges using the zigzag setting on your sewing machine *(Drawing D)*.

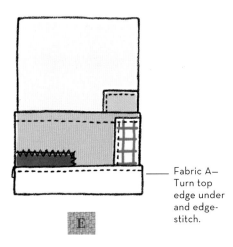

Fabric A—
Turn top
edge under
and edge-
stitch.

E

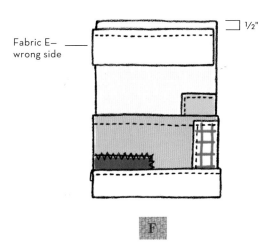

Fabric E—
wrong side

½"

F

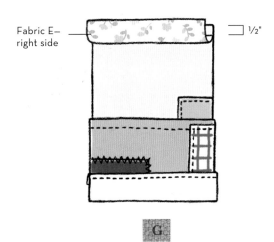

Fabric E—
right side

½"

G

Fabric A: At the bottom of the pot holder, add the 1½" x 5½" strip of undyed muslin or cotton on top of the linen, covering the bottom edge of both the red ribbon and the blue/white checked cotton. Reset your machine for a regular straight stitch, and turn under the cotton's top edge by ¼" as you edge-stitch this edge in place *(Drawing E)*.

Fabric E: With the fabrics' right sides together, pin the flower-print cotton strip to the top end of the pot holder, ½" down from the edge *(Drawing F)*. Sew the cotton in place, and flip it up so that the print's right side shows at the upper edge of the potholder *(Drawing G)*.

Decorative label: Trim the label's ends with pinking shears to give them a decorative edge and prevent fraying. Edge-stitch the label on all four sides to the front of the pot holder *(Drawing H)*.

2. Insert Hanging Loop, and Join Front and Back
With right sides together, align and pin the front and back of the pot holder together. Position the fabric or leather loop upside down at the top center in-between the front and back *(Drawing I)*. Align the cotton batting on one side of the pot holder, repinning the edges of the three layers. Sew around all four sides of the pot holder with a ⅜" seam, leaving a 2½" opening at the bottom.

Trim the corners and the selvedge edges, being careful not to cut too close to the seam. Turn the pot holder right side out through the opening at the bottom. Hand-sew the opening closed.

3. Machine-Quilt Pot Holder

To give the potholder a little extra dimension, stitch over a few previously sewn seams: on the right side of the label, across the linen, and along the vertical line of the blue vegetable-print appliqué *(Drawing J)*.

4. Fray Linen

Gently loosen the top edge of the linen (Fabric C you added in Step 1) with a needle, and carefully pull off two or three strands of the fabric's weave to fray the edge.

Note

You may want to replace the leather loop with a washable vinyl cord.

ZAKKA DESIGNER
keiko
www7.plala.or.jp/souffler

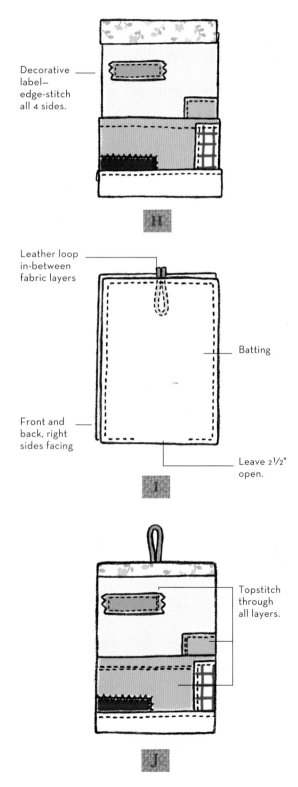

Decorative label— edge-stitch all 4 sides.

H

Leather loop in-between fabric layers

Batting

Front and back, right sides facing

Leave 2¹/₂" open.

I

Topstitch through all layers.

J

tartlet
pincushion

Keep track of your pins with this
charming pincushion that sits in
its own scalloped-edge tartlet tin.
To make it double as a hanging
ornament, you can drill a hole on
the side of the tin and attach a
hanging loop. This is a great holiday
gift for a friend who sews.

Zakka Fact

The Japanese celebrate the
seasons in many ways—for
example, with cherry blossom
festivals in the spring and
harvest moon celebrations in
the fall. They also like to
change zakka items with the
season, as part of the tradition
of *koromo-gae*, which means
literally "a seasonal change of
clothing" but also refers to a
seasonal change in household
goods. This pincushion is
perfect for winter since its
colors poetically reference the
snow and darkening days of
the season. To make a spring
pincushion, use pastel colors
and embellish with a flower
button instead of a snowflake.

Level of Difficulty

- -

Finished Size
2¾" in diameter

Materials
5"-square scrap of white wool
    or wool felt, cut in a circle,
    4¾" in diameter
3 small seed pearl beads
1 small, flat snowflake button
All-purpose white thread
Hand-sewing needle
Brioche baking tin cup,
    2¾" in diameter
Fiberfill
White glue

OPTIONAL: *Electric drill,*
embroidery floss, and bell
(for making pincushion into
hanging ornament)

- -

Seam Allowance
¼"

1. Gather Fabric into Pouch

Machine- or hand-sew a line of gathering stitches (see page 14) 1/4" from the edge of the cut fabric circle, stitching around the entire circle and leaving thread tails at the beginning and end of your stitching. Pull the thread tails gently to create a loose pouch shape, but do not knot the thread yet *(Drawing A)*.

2. Add Decorative Beads

Thread your hand-sewing needle, and knot the thread. Then insert the needle from the fabric's wrong side, and stitch the pearl beads to the front of the fabric in an off-center cluster (you can stitch from one bead to the next on the back of the fabric, and knot off when you've finished attaching the third bead). Then knot your thread again, come up from the back of the fabric, and attach a snowflake button or any other small, flat decoration you like.

3. Stuff and Finish Pincushion

Stuff the pincushion with fiberfill, pulling the thread tails slightly as you stuff and adding enough stuffing to make the pincushion rounded and firm. Then pull the thread tails tightly together, and knot off the thread.

Dab a few dots of glue on the underside of the pincushion and a few more dots of glue on the inside of the brioche tin. Set the pincushion into the tin, press it firmly, and let the glue dry.

Notes

As an alternative to using a snowflake button, you can embroider a snowflake with a backstitch (see page 11) in a thread color that contrasts with the fabric. Use the template provided at right as a stitching guide *(Drawing B)*.

If you want to transform this pincushion into a hanging ornament: Before gluing the pincushion into the brioche tin, use an electric drill with a thin drill bit (the designer used a 1/8" bit) to make a small hole about 1/4" from the top edge of one of the tin's flutes. Thread a strand of embroidery floss or a very narrow ribbon through the drilled hole, even up the length of the two ends of floss or ribbon, thread the two ends together though the ring on the tiny bell, knot the ends together, and hang your ornament.

ZAKKA DESIGNER
shinobee
www18.ocn.ne.jp/~chou/

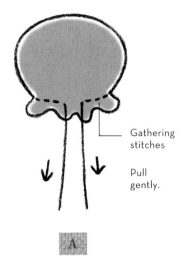

Gathering stitches

Pull gently.

A

SNOWFLAKE TEMPLATE
(at actual size)

B

bunko-bon book cover

In many Japanese cities, people commute to work on public transportation. Young women often cover their *bunko-bon* (small paperback book) with a handmade textile cozy, or cover. If you last made a book cover in high school, now is the time to upgrade your skills.

Zakka Fact

In Japan paperback books are all the same size, $4\frac{1}{8}$" x $5\frac{7}{8}$". Making a cover for one's *bunko-bon* is a popular pastime—and another example of the Japanese tendency to cover things and make them neat. It's also a way to show off your sense of style while keeping your reading material private.

Level of Difficulty

- -

Finished Size

9¼" x 6½" *(opened flat)*;
4⅝" x 6½" *(folded)*
Fits book 4⅛" x 5⅞" x ¾"
    *(see information about
    adjusting book cover's size at
    end of instructions)*

- -

Materials

Fabric A: Scrap of red/white
    printed linen, 7" x 11¾"
    (for outside book cover)
Fabric B: Scrap of large white
    polka-dotted red linen, 7" x
    11¾" *(for lining)*
Fabric C: Scrap of small white
    polka-dotted red cotton,
    1⅛" x 3¾" *(for embellishment)*

10" length of ¼"-wide ribbon
    *(for bookmark; we used linen
    tape ribbon)*
Tiny scrap of red/white ribbon,
    about ⅜" x ¾" *(for book
    mark's tip; ribbon tip should be
    slightly wider than bookmark
    ribbon to give it some weight)*
All-purpose sewing thread to
    match linen

- -

Seam allowance

¼"

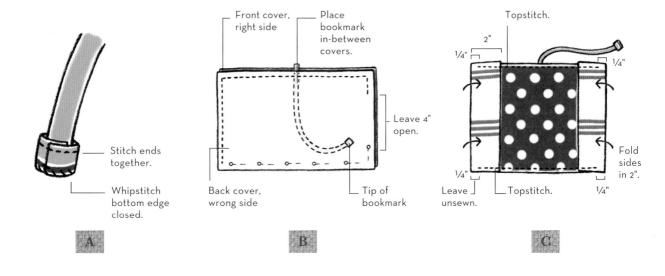

Stitch ends together.

Whipstitch bottom edge closed.

A

Front cover, right side

Place bookmark in-between covers.

Leave 4" open.

Back cover, wrong side

Tip of bookmark

B

Topstitch.

2"

1/4"

1/4"

1/4"

Leave unsewn.

Topstitch.

1/4"

Fold sides in 2".

C

1. Make Bookmark

Center one end of the bookmark ribbon in the middle of the red/white bookmark-tip ribbon. Fold the ribbon tip's ends over the bookmark, tucking under the raw edge of the end on top, and stitch the ends in place. Take a couple of whipstitches (see page 15) along the bottom edge to hold the ribbon in place (*Drawing A*).

2. Sew Book Cover

With the fabrics' right sides together and the edges aligned, pin Fabric A to Fabric B, sandwiching the bookmark between the two pieces at the center top edge and making sure that the bookmark's uncovered end is positioned at the seam allowances (*Drawing B*).

Machine-baste (see page 9) the book-cover sandwich in place. Then sew it together, stitching around all four sides of the sandwich 1/4" from the edge and leaving a 4" opening on one short side (*Drawing B*).

Trim the four corners and turn the book cover right side out through the opening. Fold and press the fabric edges under at the opening and topstitch (see page 10) the opening closed.

3. Fold Sides in to Make Pockets

Fold in and pin each short side of the cover 2" toward the lining to form a pocket.

Topstitch the book cover's top and bottom edges to secure the folds, starting and stopping 1/4" from each outside edge, as shown in *Drawing C*, to provide space for a book to fit into the cover.

Note

To make a book cover that fits a different-size book, lay your closed book on a flat surface and measure its width. Double that measurement and add the width of the book's spine. Then add 4 1/2" to *that* measurement (for the side pockets and the 1/4" seam allowances) to get your final width measurement. Measure the book's length from top to bottom and add 1". Cut your fabric to these dimensions and follow the directions above to make the cover.

ZAKKA DESIGNER
Kui Hazuki
http://drops.cheap.jp/

linen basket

Filled with small sewing items
like spools of thread, a seam ripper,
and tailor's chalk, this linen basket
makes a lovely gift for your favorite
crafter. If desired, it's easy to
enlarge the pattern to make a bigger
basket for holding bulkier items. For
a personal touch, add a button or
embroider a design referring to the
items you'll place inside.

Zakka Fact

Bamboo basket-making
is a traditional craft in Japan.
Today modern DIYers are
reviving the tradition with
a twist by sewing fabric
baskets and using them for
utilitarian purposes or for
display. For example, they
might stitch a basket in
which to display clothespins
in a laundry area or room
shoes (see page 118) at the
entrance to a home.

Level of Difficulty

Finished Size
4" square x 3½" high

Materials
Scrap of linen, cut 12" square
Scrap of printed cotton,
    cut 12" square
1 decorative button, 1" in diameter
Scrap of cotton batting, 12" square
All-purpose thread in red, cream,
    and tan *(to match linen)*
Linen Basket pattern *(see page 37)*

Preparing the Fabric
CUT USING PATTERN
Linen: 1 basket
Print fabric: 1 basket
Cotton batting: 1 basket

CUT FREEHAND
Linen: 2 pieces, 2" x 5" *(for
handles)*

Seam Allowance
¼"

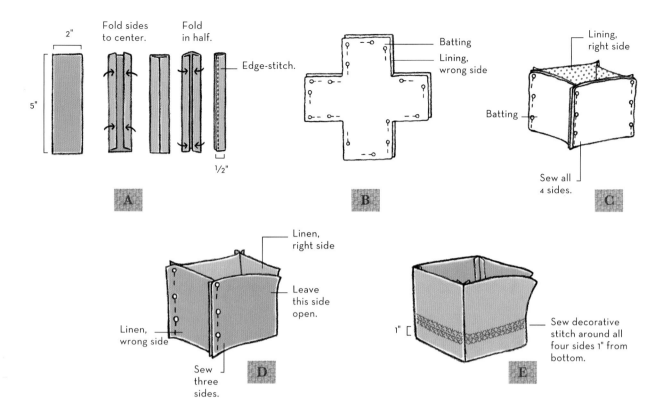

1. Make Handles

To make the first handle, lay one 2" x 5" linen rectangle wrong side up, and fold and press the two long edges so they meet in the center. Fold and press the strip in half lengthwise so that it's ½" wide. Then edge-stitch (see page 10) the folded fabric along its length *(Drawing A)*.

Repeat to make the second handle and set both aside.

2. Construct Lining

With the printed lining fabric wrong side up, align and pin the cotton batting to the lining *(Drawing B)*. Using cream thread in your machine, baste (see page 9) the pair together, stitching around them ¼" from the edge.

With the batting on the outside and the lining fabric's right sides together, pin the sides of the basket together *(Drawing C)*. Then sew each side seam with a ¼" seam, and set the lining basket aside.

3. Construct Linen Basket

With the fabric's right sides together, align and pin the sides of the cut linen piece to form a basket. With tan thread in your machine, sew three of the sides with a ¼" seam, and leave the fourth side unsewn *(Drawing D)*. Turn the basket right side out. Using red thread in your machine and working on the right side of the basket, sew a decorative stitch around the

basket's four sides about 1" from the bottom *(Drawing E)*. (See the template detail in *Drawing F* on page 36 for this stitch, and the note at the end of the project for ideas for alternative stitches). Start stitching at one raw edge of the basket's open side, and continue around the other sides, maintaining the 1" distance from the bottom, so your stitches will match up on the final side.

After completing the decorative stitching, turn the basket wrong side out, and sew the last side seam to close the open side.

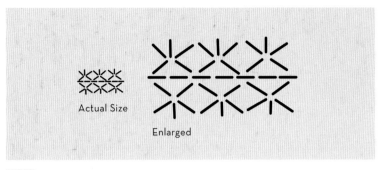

Actual Size

Enlarged

 Decorative Stitch Template

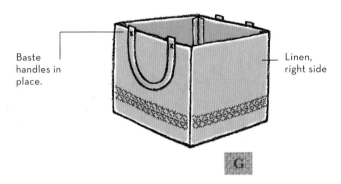

Baste handles in place.

Linen, right side

G

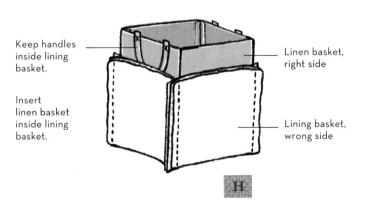

Keep handles inside lining basket.

Insert linen basket inside lining basket.

Linen basket, right side

Lining basket, wrong side

H

Pin the handles upside down on opposing sides of the linen basket, with the two ends of each handle equidistant from the side seams, as shown in *Drawing G*. Baste the handles in place.

4. Join Lining and Basket
With the print lining basket wrong side out and the linen basket right side out, place the linen basket inside the lining basket *(Drawing H)*. Make sure that the basket's handles are sandwiched between the right sides of both fabrics.

Stitch around the top edge on three sides ¼" from the edge, leaving the fourth side open for turning *(Drawing I)*. Turn the basket right side out, and whipstitch (see page 15) the open top edge closed by hand *(Drawing J)*.

5. Add Decorative Button
Hand-sew a decorative button on the front of the basket, placing it off-center.

Note
If your sewing machine doesn't have the decorative stitch used on this basket, you can create a similar look with a double-zigzag stitch. Alternatively, decorate the basket with a narrow ribbon or rickrack.

ZAKKA DESIGNER
sayaka suzuki
http://plaza.across.or.jp/~szkms/

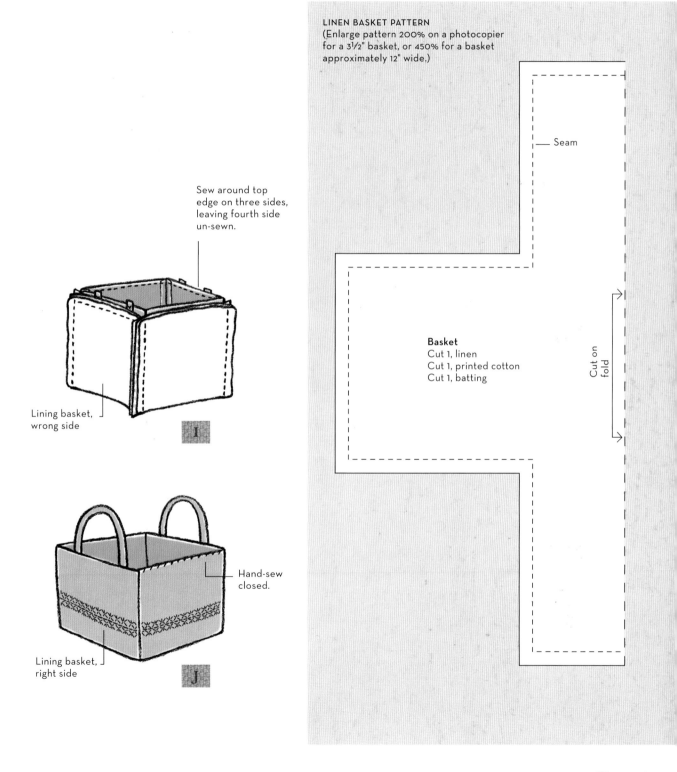

Sew around top edge on three sides, leaving fourth side un-sewn.

Lining basket, wrong side

I

Hand-sew closed.

Lining basket, right side

J

LINEN BASKET PATTERN
(Enlarge pattern 200% on a photocopier for a 3½" basket, or 450% for a basket approximately 12" wide.)

Seam

Basket
Cut 1, linen
Cut 1, printed cotton
Cut 1, batting

Cut on fold

tape
measure cozy

Making your utilitarian tape measure really *kawaii* (cute) can be as simple as adding a cozy to cover it. The fabric circle charms are an additional decorative touch reminiscent of the cell phone charms that originated in Japan. Complete your cozy with a pincushion or needle case in matching fabric.

Zakka Fact

Japanese tend to wrap many everyday items in textile covers, which keeps them neat and clean—and, of course, makes them cute!

Level of Difficulty

- -

Finished Size
2¼" square x ¾" deep;
    string of charms, 2½" long

Materials
Fabric A: Scrap of printed cotton,
    6" x 12"
Fabrics B, C, and D: Small scraps
    of printed cotton, about
    2" square *(for circle charms)*
Fabric E: Scrap of printed cotton,
    2" x 2½" *(for pull loop)*
2" length of ⅟₁₆"-wide nylon cord
Cotton batting
All-purpose sewing thread
    to match fabric
Hand-sewing needle
Purchased tape measure,
    2" square
White glue
Cozy Cover pattern
    (see facing page)

Preparing the Fabric
CUT USING PATTERN
Fabric A: 4 covers
    (2 for front and 2 for back)
Cotton batting: 2 covers

CUT FREEHAND
Fabric A: 2 pieces, 1¼" x 5";
    2 pieces, 1¼" x 4⅛"
Fabrics B, C, and D: 2 circles of
    each fabric, ¾" in diameter
Fabric E: 1 piece, 2" x 2½"
Cotton batting: 1 piece, 1¼" x 5";
    1 piece, 1¼" x 4⅛"; 3 circles,
    ¾" in diameter

- -

Seam Allowance
¼"

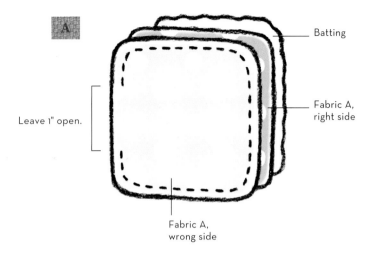

A

Batting

Leave 1" open.

Fabric A, right side

Fabric A, wrong side

COZY COVER PATTERN
(Enlarge pattern 200% on a photocopier.)

Cozy Cover
Cut 4, Fabric A
Cut 2, batting

Seam

1. Make Front and Back Covers

You'll construct this cozy by machine-sewing all the individual parts as directed in Steps 1-3 and then hand-sewing the parts together to cover the tape measure.

To make the front cover, place two of the cut covers with right sides together and the edges aligned, and pin a matching piece of cotton batting on top. Machine-sew this fabric-and-batting sandwich together, stitching around the square with a ¼" seam and leaving a 1" opening on one side *(Drawing A)*.

Turn the cover right side out through the opening, and press it. Hand-sew the opening closed with a whipstitch (see page 15), and set the front cover aside.

Repeat to make the back cover.

2. Make Side Panels

Using the freehand-cut pieces of Fabric A and the matching strips of batting, repeat the process in Step 1 to make the cozy's two long side panels. Set them aside.

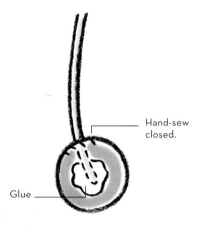

Hand-sew closed.

Glue

B

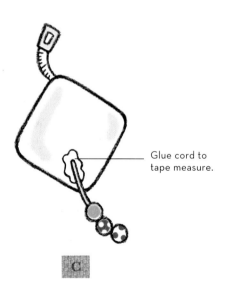

Glue cord to tape measure.

C

3. Make Circle Charms

Place the two Fabric B circles together with the right sides together, and pin a batting circle on one side of the pair. Machine-sew around the circle, $1/4"$ from the edge, leaving a $1/2"$ opening. Turn the circle right side out through the opening, press the circle, and hand-sew the opening closed with a whipstitch. Repeat the process with the Fabric C circles to make the second charm.

For the third charm (the one closest to the tape measure), repeat the process above with the Fabric D circles up to the point of turning the charm right side out. Then dab a little bit of glue inside the charm. Insert one end of the nylon cord into the glue inside the charm, and let the glue dry (*Drawing B*). Whipstitch the opening closed, being careful to secure the cord inside the charm.

Sew the three circle charms together, end to end, using a few hand stitches to catch them one-to-another.

4. Construct Cozy

Glue the nylon cord to the side of the tape measure (at the corner opposite the pull tab) *(Drawing C)*. Pin the sewn front and back covers and side panels around the tape measure *(Drawing D)*. Whipstitch the covers to the side panels, and stitch across the seam where the nylon cord is attached.

5. Make Pull Tab

With Fabric E rectangle laid wrong side up, fold and press its long edges in, so they meet at center. Fold and press the rectangle again in half lengthwise, and hand-sew the long side together.

Slip the fabric pull tab through the slot on the tape measure's pull tab, and tuck one end of the fabric tab into the other end, turning under the raw edge of the outer end. Hand-sew the tab's ends together *(Drawing E)*.

Note

You can substitute string, yarn, several strands of embroidery floss, or a narrow ribbon for the nylon cord attaching the circle charms to the tape measure.

ZAKKA DESIGNER
noboru
http://handmade-pommier.ciao.jp/hp-pommier/

Tape measure

Pin and hand-sew cover around tape measure.

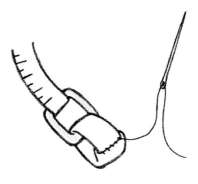

Hand-sew ends closed.

pear purse

"This pear is delicious, isn't it?"—
or so says the phrase embroidered on
this purse. The unusual round shape
and cute appliqué make this project as
pretty as it is practical.

Zakka Fact

Fruit and foreign words
and phrases are both
popular motifs in zakka
design. This purse is
a great example of both
of these design elements.

Level of Difficulty

Finished Size

Purse, 8" in diameter x 1¾" deep;
   handle, 14" long

Materials

Fabric A: ½ yard linen twill
   (for outside),
Fabric B: ½ yard printed cotton
   (for lining),
Fabric C, D, and E: Scraps of
   cotton, about 2" x 5"
   (for appliqués)
½ yard cotton batting
Embroidery floss in yellow, green,
   brown, and grey-blue
All-purpose thread to match linen
Hand-sewing needle
Embroidery needle
Water-soluble disappearing-ink pen
Pear Appliqué patterns
   (see facing page)

Preparing the Fabric

CUT USING PATTERN
Fabric C: Pear pattern
Fabric D: Reverse of pear pattern
Fabric E: 1 pear leaf

CUT FREEHAND
Fabric A: 2 circles, 9" in diameter
   (for purse front and back);
   1 piece, 2½" x 21" *(for side
   band);* 1 piece, 2¾" x 15"
   (for handle)
Fabric B: 2 circles, 9" in diameter;
   1 piece, 2½" x 21"; 1 piece, 2¾" x
   15"
Cotton batting: 2 circles, 9" in
   diameter; 1 piece, 2 ½" x 21";
   1 piece, 2¾" x 15"

Seam Allowance

½"

1. Appliqué Pear on Purse

Referring to the photograph on the facing page, position and pin the pear halves on the front of the purse, overlapping them slightly at the center seam. Using an embroidery needle and a strand or two of the green and yellow embroidery floss as needed to match the fabric, blanket-stitch (see page 12) around the outside of the pear and down its center.

Using the brown floss, embroider stem with long, vertical satin stitches (see page 15).

Finally, using the grey-blue floss, pin the cut leaf by the stem, and blanket-stitch around it.

2. Embroider Phrase on Purse

Use the template below and a water-soluble disappearing-ink pen to transfer the lettering to the front of the purse (see page 8). Then, using a doubled strand of brown floss and a backstitch (see page 11), embroider the lettering on the purse front (see the photo on the facing page for positioning).

PEAR APPLIQUÉ PATTERNS
(at actual size)

Leaf
Cut 1, Fabric E

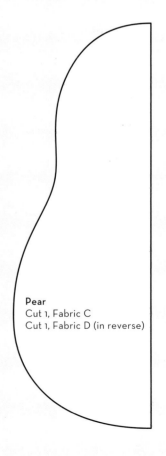

Pear
Cut 1, Fabric C
Cut 1, Fabric D (in reverse)

PHRASE TEMPLATE
(at actual size)

Cette poire est delicieuse, n'est-ce pas?

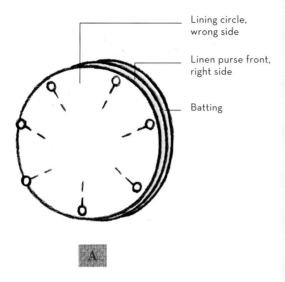

Lining circle,
wrong side

Linen purse front,
right side

Batting

A

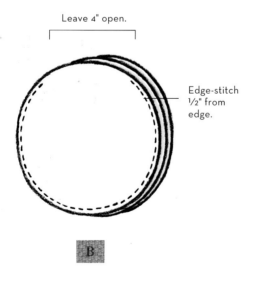

Leave 4" open.

Edge-stitch
½" from
edge.

B

3. Make Purse Front and Back

Place and align the embellished purse front, right side up, on top of one of the batting circles. Then place and align one printed lining circle, wrong side up, on top of the purse front and pin the three layers in place *(Drawing A)*. With the linen-colored thread in your sewing machine, stitch all three layers together, sewing ½" from the edge and leaving a 4" opening at the top center of the purse for the handle *(Drawing B)*.

Repeat the process above to make the purse back. Then turn both the purse front and back right side out through the openings, press, and set aside.

4. Make Side Panel

Place and align the linen side panel, right side up, on top of the batting side panel. Then place and align the printed lining side panel, wrong side up, on the top of the linen and pin the trio together. Stitch the trio along the long sides and one of the short sides, sewing ½" from the edge and leaving the second short side unsewn. Clip the corners, turn the side panel right side out through the opening, and press it. Hand-sew the opening closed, and set the panel aside.

5. Make Handle

Using the pieces you cut for the handle, repeat Step 4 to make the handle and set it aside.

6. Sew Purse Together

With the lining sides facing together, pin the side panel to the purse front and back, making sure the appliqué and embroidery on the front are straight. Edge-stitch ⅛" from the edge around the purse circle, sewing only the side panel in place and leaving the top center of the circle unstitched *(Drawing C)*.

7. Attach Handle

Insert each end of the handle into the center top opening on each side of the purse, as shown in *Drawing C*. Hand-sew the opening closed, securely attaching the handle *(Drawing D)*.

ZAKKA DESIGNER
powa*powa*
http://powa-powa.com/

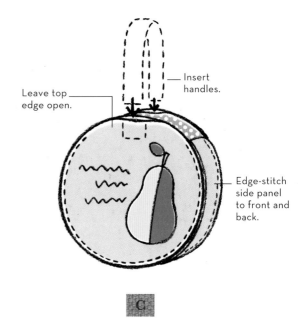

Leave top edge open.

Insert handles.

Edge-stitch side panel to front and back.

C

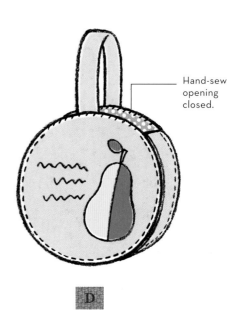

Hand-sew opening closed.

D

cross
tote bag

Elegant and simple, this
tote is classically stylish. The
wool fabric makes it a great
choice for fall and winter.
Make another one for spring
and summer in bright white
linen with tulips appliquéd
across the front.

Zakka Fact

Seasons change, and so
should your zakka.
Japanese zakka designers
change motifs, colors, and
fabrics with each season.

Level of Difficulty

- -

Finished Size

10½" x 12½"; handles, 16" long

Materials

½ yard brown heather wool
  (for front and back of tote)
½ yard beige cotton twill or
  flannel (for lining and pocket)
Cream wool felt, 8½" x 11"
  (for cross appliqués)
¾"-wide leather, 32" length cut
  into two 16" pieces (for straps)
16 nail heads (for attaching
  handles)
All-purpose thread in brown
  and beige
Embroidery floss in red and
  cream
Embroidery needle
Cross Appliqué pattern
  (see page 55)

Preparing the Fabric

CUT USING PATTERN
Cream wool felt: 6 crosses

CUT FREEHAND
Brown wool: 2 pieces, 11½" x 13½"
Beige cotton twill: 2 pieces,
  11½" x 13½"; 1 piece, 7½" x 10"

- -

Seam Allowance

½"

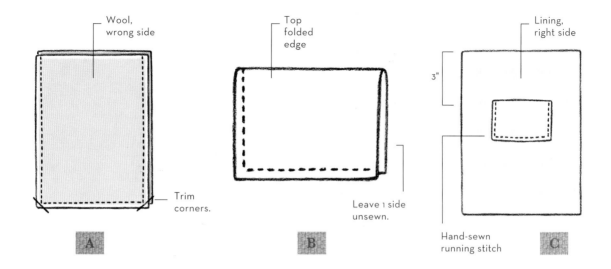

Wool, wrong side

Trim corners.

A

Top folded edge

Leave 1 side unsewn.

B

Lining, right side

3"

Hand-sewn running stitch

C

1. Appliqué Crosses to Front of Bag

Pin the six felt crosses in place on one of the brown wool pieces, referring to the photograph on page 51 for positioning. Then hand-embroider each cross on the wool, using a whipstitch (see page 15) and cream-colored floss in your embroidery needle.

2. Make Tote Bag

With the fabrics' right sides facing, pin the front and back of the tote bag together. Using all-purpose brown thread in your machine, stitch the front and back together along the long sides and the bottom edge with a ¹/₂" seam, leaving the top of the bag open. Trim the bottom corners *(Drawing A)*. Then press the seams open, turn the bag right side out, and set it aside.

3. Make Interior Pocket

Fold the small cotton twill rectangle for the pocket in half, matching the short edges. With all-purpose beige thread in your machine, stitch along one side and the bottom edge, leaving the last side open *(Drawing B)*. Note that the top of the pocket will be the fold of the fabric and does not need to be stitched.

Turn the pocket right side out, fold under the edges of the opening, and hand-sew it closed.

4. Attach Pocket to Lining

Place the pocket on the right side of one of the lining pieces 3" down from the top edge and centered, and pin it in place. Using red embroidery floss and a running stitch (see page 14), hand-sew the pocket to the lining ¹/₈" in from the pocket's edge, stitching down one side, across the bottom, and up the other side. Leave the top open *(Drawing C)*.

5. Sew Lining

With the right sides facing, pin the lining front and back together, and stitch around the sides and bottom with a ¹/₂" seam. Trim the bottom corners, and press the seams open.

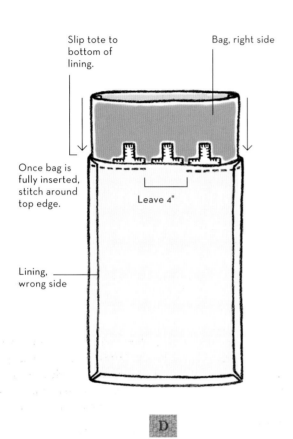

Slip tote to bottom of lining.

Bag, right side

Once bag is fully inserted, stitch around top edge.

Leave 4"

Lining, wrong side

D

Attach leather handles with nail heads.

E

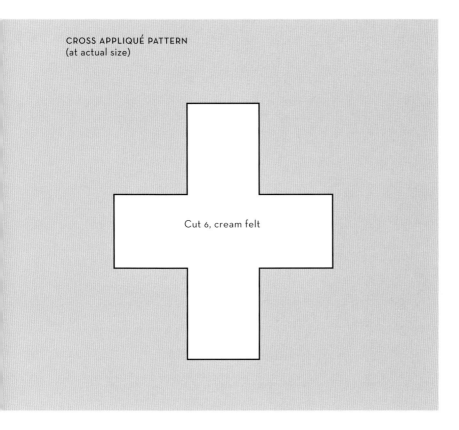

CROSS APPLIQUÉ PATTERN
(at actual size)

Cut 6, cream felt

6. Sew Bag Together

With the wool bag right side out and the lining wrong side out, slip the wool bag inside the lining *(Drawing D)*. Stitch around the bag's top edge with a ¹⁄₂" seam, leaving a 4" opening on one side. Turn the tote right side out, and stitch the opening closed by hand using a slipstitch (see page 15).

7. Attach Handles

The designer chose a heavy leather strap for the handles, which require nail heads for attaching them to the bag (see Resources on page 151) *(Drawing E)*. Alternatively, you could choose a different material for the handles, such as thin leather, vinyl, or webbing trim. Cut the strap material into two strips ³⁄₄" x 16", and hand-sew them on the right side of the tote front and back with a glover's hand-sewing needle, heavy thread, and ¹⁄₂"-long running stitches (see page 14) as follows: Sew a 1"-long running-stitch box at the base of each handle and a large running-stitch 'X' inside each box.

Optional

If desired, add a decorative label to the interior pocket by writing with permanent fabric marker or embroidering on some cotton twill tape and sewing it to the pocket.

ZAKKA DESIGNER
massimo
http://www8.ocn.ne.
jp/~massimo/

coat cover

- -

A "green" alternative to plastic garment
bags, this lovely linen garment cover
protects your coats and party dresses
until you need them for the next
season or event.

Zakka Fact

With small living spaces
and a design aesthetic
that celebrates clean lines,
Japanese culture places
a high value on items
that keep environments
tidy. A protective cover
for your clothing is both
popular and practical.

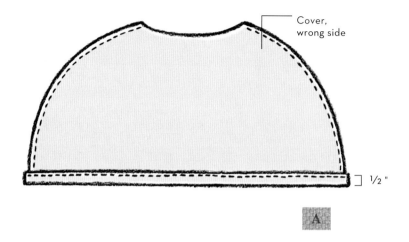

Cover,
wrong side

½ "

A

Level of Difficulty

- -

Finished Size

26" (at base) x 15½"

Materials

1 yard 36"-wide linen
53" length 1"-wide lace trim
All-purpose thread to match linen
Straightedge ruler
Large piece of paper to make
    a pattern
OPTIONAL: Decorative fabric label

- -

Making a Pattern and Preparing the Fabric

Place a large piece of paper, such as a brown-paper grocery bag opened out flat, on a flat surface, and lay the shoulders of your coat on top of the paper. Trace from the garment's neck/collar around the edge of the shoulders and down about 10" along the sleeves (or more if you want a longer cover).

Add a generous 2" to the entire traced outline to allow for the thickness of the coat—more if your coat is bulky—and use the ruler to connect the two bottom points at the sleeves with a straight horizontal line. Draw a gently curved line at the top/neck edge connecting the outline's two top points; this will become the opening for the hanger. Cut the pattern from the paper. With the linen fabric laid out flat, cut 2 pieces using the pattern you just created.

- -

Seam Allowance

½"

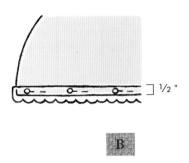

⌐ ½ "

B

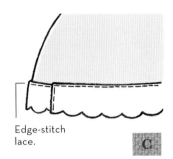

Edge-stitch
lace.

C

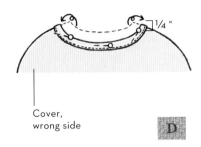

¼ "

Cover,
wrong side

D

1. Sew Coat Cover

Lay the two cut covers on top
of one another with their edges
aligned. Sew the pair along the
curving side seams with a ½"
seam allowance, backstitching
(see page 11) at the beginning
and end of the seam.

Keeping the cover wrong side out,
fold the bottom raw edge ½"
to the wrong side and press the
folded edge with a hot iron.
Turn this folded edge another
½" to the wrong side, and press
the double fold.

Pin the bottom hem in place;
and, working on the fabric's
wrong side, topstitch (see page
10) along the hem's upper
fold *(Drawing A)*.

2. Add Lace to Hem

Turn the coat cover right
side out and pin the lace on
the fabric's right side across
the bottom edge, positioning the
lace's top edge ½" from the
cover's bottom edge and one of
the lace's ends near one of the
cover's side seams *(Drawing B)*.

When you arrive back where you
started pinning, fold under the
last end of the lace ½" and pin
this end over the other end by
½". Edge-stitch (see page 10) the
lace's top edge to the coat cover,
sewing from the lace's overlapped
bottom edge up to the lace's top
edge and then, with the needle
down, pivoting the corner so you
can stitch along the lace's upper
edge around the cover *(Drawing
C)*. Backstitch at the beginning
and end of your seam.

3. Finish Neckline

With the cover wrong side out,
turn the neck edge ¼" to the
wrong side. Press the folded edge.
Turn this edge another ¼" to the
wrong side, press again, and pin
the double fold in place. Then
topstitch the double fold from the
wrong side ¼" from the edge
(Drawing D).

Note

If you want to add a decorative
label, make your own or purchase
a decorative twill tape or ribbon
to use as a label. You could also
attach a small pocket to the cover
and stuff it with lavender to keep
your garment smelling fresh.

ZAKKA DESIGNER
Reiko
http://www002.upp.so-net.
ne.jp/ete/index.htm

house
camera cozy

If you're a little protective of your
new small digital camera, consider
making this adorable cozy, which
fits most point-and-shoot models
with a little room to spare. This piece
also tells a story: On rainy days,
Japanese children are encouraged
to make a little white doll that looks
like a ghost. Called *teruteru-bozu*
(sunshine boy), the doll is hung in
the window as a charm to make
the rain stop so the children can go
out and play. Open the door on
the front of the cozy, and you'll see
a little girl waiting patiently for the
sun to shine.

Zakka Fact:

In Japan, everything
needs a cozy, or
cover—especially
electronic equipment.

Level of Difficulty

- -

Finished Size

3⅝" x 5" x 1"; strap, 10" long

- -

Materials

FABRIC

Scrap of beige cotton twill,
    7½" x 12"
Scrap of brown cotton twill,
    4" x 5¼"
Scrap of red denim, 2" x 2½"
Scrap of beige-polka-dotted
    red cotton, 5" x 6"
Scrap of red-polka-dotted
    beige cotton, 7" x 12"

Scrap of white-polka-dotted
    beige cotton, 1" x 3"
Scrap of white-polka-dotted
    pink cotton, 3" x 2½"
Scrap of white-striped pink
    cotton, 2" x 2½"
Scrap of white cotton, 1½" square
Scrap of blue chambray, 1" x 1¼"
    (for behind window)
Scrap of white-polka-dotted
    orange cotton, 1" x 1½"
    (for loop for clasp)
Scrap of red felt, 1" x 2"
Scrap of moss green felt, 1" x 4"
Scrap of white felt, 1" square
Scrap of light pink felt, 1" square
Scrap of pale yellow felt, 1" square
Scrap of grey felt, 1" square

TRIM

Embroidery floss in brown, beige,
    red, moss green, yellow,
    and pink
Five ³/₁₆" buttons
One ¼" button

One ³/₁₆" wooden bead
    (for doorknob)
8" length of small pompom trim
½" of dark red waxed cotton
    thread or thick string
    (for door latch)

OTHER MATERIALS

Thin cotton batting, 5" x 11"
Two ⅝" lengths ⅜"-wide Velcro
Metal snap-bolt clasp
Fiberfill (tiny amount)
Embroidery needle
All-purpose sewing thread
    in beige
White glue
House Camera Cozy patterns
    (see page 67)

Preparing the Fabric

CUT USING PATTERNS

Beige cotton twill: 1 house

Brown cotton twill: 1 bottom

Red denim: 1 door

Beige-polka-dotted red cotton:
  2 roofs

Red-polka-dotted beige cotton:
  1 house lining

White-polka-dotted pink cotton:
  1 door

White-striped pink cotton: 1 door

Red felt: 1 hooded girl

Moss green felt: 2 grasses
  (cut off 1 leaf on 1 cut grass)

White felt: 1 bird

Pink felt: 1 bird (trim cut bird by
  1/8" all around)

Yellow felt: 1 butterfly

Cotton batting: 1 house (trim off
  all 1/2" seam allowances)

CUT FREEHAND

Beige cotton twill: 1 piece,
  1 3/8" x 11 1/2" (for handle)

White cotton: 1 circle, 1 1/4" in
  diameter (for *teruteru-bozu*
  hanging doll)

Pink felt: 1 circle, 1/4" in diameter
  (for girl's face)

Grey felt: 1 half circle, 1/4" in
  diameter (for girl's hair)

- -

Seam allowance:
3/8"

1. Prepare House

Lay the beige twill house wrong side up. Place the cotton batting on top and baste together.

2. Make Door

Prepare door's "background": With the white polka-dotted pink-cotton door wrong side up, make tiny notches (1/8" or less) into its curved top edge, and turn and press all the door's edges 1/4" to the wrong side.

With the beige twill house right side up, center the white polka-dotted pink-cotton door on one side of the house, 3" down from the roof's top edge. Pin the door in place *(Drawing A)*.

Make door "latch": Make a loop of the dark red waxed-cotton thread, being sure that it fits around the wooden bead you'll use for the doorknob and trimming the extra length of the doubled thread ends to about 1/4" long. Dab the thread ends with a bit of glue and insert them under the left side of the white polka-dotted pink-cotton door, so the "latch" extends from the door. Slipstitch (see page 15) around the door background to attach it and the door latch to the house, and set the house aside.

Make and attach outer red door: Using brown floss in your embroidery needle, hand-sew a star (sew a couple of straight stitches, crossing one another) on the front of the red denim door. Then align the red door and the white-striped pink door, with right sides together, and pin the two in place. Using the all-purpose thread in your machine, stitch the pair together with a 1/4" seam, leaving the bottom edge unsewn. Turn the door right side out through the opening, and sew the opening closed by hand.

Place the red door on top of the white polka-dotted pink-cotton door background, and slipstitch the two together along the right edge of the doors.

Sew the wooden-bead doorknob on the door's left side, positioning it to match up with the door latch you added above.

Embellish door's background: Glue the red felt girl to the white polka-dotted pink background. Glue the pink felt face on the girl, and add the tiny scrap of grey felt for her hair. Using brown and pink floss, embroider eyes and a mouth with a couple of straight stitches. Then use brown floss to sew a couple of crossing straight stitches to make a star in the middle of the girl's red dress.

Red Door

Hanging Doll
Embroider eyes and
mouth before stuffing
head and hanging.

 Cozy Elements in Place with Details

3. Make Window

Cut the window out of the other side of the beige cotton twill house (see *Drawing A* for the window's placement). Center the blue chambray window, right side up, behind the opening and pin it in place. Working from the right side of the house and using beige floss, sew a running stitch (see page 14) around the window ⅛" from its edge, attaching the blue background to the window. Glue the pink and white birds in the window (*Drawing A*), and decorate them with a few embroidered straight stitches to make eyes and beaks.

4. Add Butterfly and Grass

Lightly glue the grass pieces on both sides of the house (*Drawing A*). Add a few embroidered backstitches (see page 11) in moss green floss to simulate veins in the leaves.

Lightly glue the butterfly to the upper right of the window (see *Drawing A*), and use yellow floss to secure it with a couple of straight stitches in the center. Using beige floss, add a French knot (see page 13) to each of the butterfly's wings. And with moss green floss and a running stitch, embroider a line under the butterfly simulating her flight path (to enliven her flight path, switch to another color of floss in the middle of it, then return to moss green to finish it).

5. Add Flower Buttons

Sew the buttons on the front and back of the house to make flowers, and add a few backstitches with moss green floss to simulate the stems (*Drawing A*).

6. Add Star Embroidery

Using brown floss, sew a few crossing straight stitches to make a star over the door and another over the window.

7. Make Roof

With the house right side up, baste (see page 9) the pompom trim on the roofline of the house on each end. With the roof pieces wrong side up, align and pin one roof to the front of the house, laying its bottom edge across the top end of the pompom trim (*Drawing B*), and pin the second roof in the same position on the back of the house. Edge-stitch (see page 10) along each roof line to attach the two roofs to the house. Then flip both roof pieces up to show their right side, and baste each roof to the house along its top edges.

8. Attach Bottom to House
With the house right side up, lay the brown twill house bottom, right side up, on top of the house, aligning the edges. Pin the house bottom in place.

Using red floss, blanket-stitch (see page 12) across the house bottom's long straight edges. Baste the remaining edges to the house *(Drawing C)*.

9. Make Loop for Clasp
With the white polka-dotted orange fabric wrong side up, fold and press its long sides ¼" to the center. Then fold and press the piece in half lengthwise, and edge-stitch the long side closed.

Make a loop of the fabric, and edgestitch the loop to the left side of the roof *(Drawing D)*.

10. Sew Lining to House
With the red polka-dotted beige house lining right side up, sew each half of the Velcro to the house lining (see the pattern for placement).

With right sides facing, pin both of the roof edges to the lining (see *Drawing E*), and stitch the pieces together along the roof edge only.

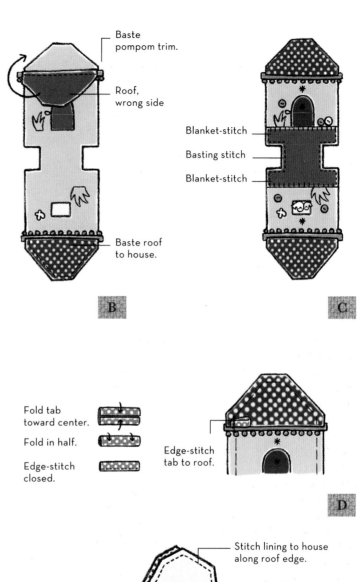

Baste pompom trim.

Roof, wrong side

Baste roof to house.

B

Blanket-stitch

Basting stitch

Blanket-stitch

C

Fold tab toward center.

Fold in half.

Edge-stitch closed.

Edge-stitch tab to roof.

D

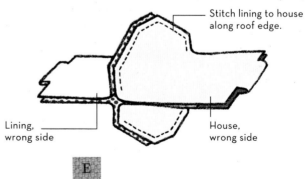

Stitch lining to house along roof edge.

Lining, wrong side

House, wrong side

E

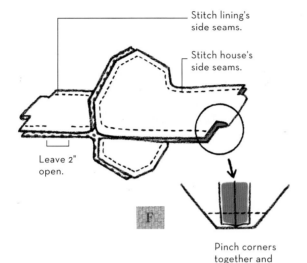

Stitch lining's
side seams.

Stitch house's
side seams.

Leave 2"
open.

F

Pinch corners
together and
stitch across.

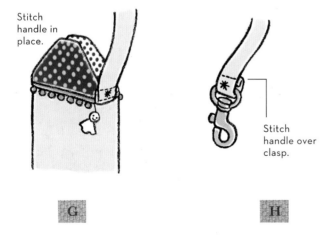

Stitch
handle in
place.

G

Stitch
handle over
clasp.

H

With right sides still together, pin the house front to the house back and the lining front to the lining back along the side seams. Stitch the side seams of, first, the house and then the lining, leaving a 2" opening in the lining (*Drawing F*). Press the seams open.

Pinch and pin each of the four bottom corners together, and stitch across each corner, as shown in *Drawing F*. Turn the house and lining right side out through the opening in the lining, and hand-sew the opening closed.

11. Make *Teruteru-Bozu* Doll
Using the moss green floss, embroider tiny eyes and a mouth on the center of the white cotton fabric circle. Using red floss, embroider a running-stitch circle about ½" in diameter around the doll's face (see *Drawing A* for placement), leaving a 4" thread tail. Do not knot off the thread.

Stuff the center of the circle with a tiny bit of fiberfill, pull the red thread tail to draw up the stitches and form the head, and knot the thread off. Tie a red-thread bow around the doll's neck.

Using a strand of beige floss, take a stitch or two in the roof line under the pompom trim on the right side of the house front (see *Drawings A* and *G* for placement), then take a stitch or two in the center of the doll's head, leaving about ¾" of thread between the doll and roof line, so the doll will dangle freely from the roof. Stitch down through the doll's head and knot off the floss on the inside of the doll's "skirt."

12. Make Handle

Begin the strap by making patchwork fabric for the underside of the handle from any combination of the polka-dotted cottons, and cut the patchwork fabric to 1⅜" by 11½".

Align and pin the patchwork handle and the cotton twill handle together, with right sides facing. Stitch their long sides together with a ⅜" seam. Then turn the handle right side out and press it flat.

Working with the handle right side up, edge-stitch both long sides to reinforce the handle. Then fold one of the handle's ends ¼" to the wrong side and, using red thread, hand-stitch it to the house's top side edge opposite the loop *(Drawing G)*.

At the strap's other end, slide the snap-bolt clasp over the fabric's edge; then turn under the strap's end ⅜", and then again ½". Hand-stitch the folded end closed *(Drawing H)*.

Using red floss, hand-sew a couple of crossing straight stitches to make a star on each end of the strap (see *Drawings G and H)*. Hook the clasp onto the loop.

ZAKKA DESIGNER
Shoko Yajima
http://www008.upp.so-net.ne.jp/yaji/

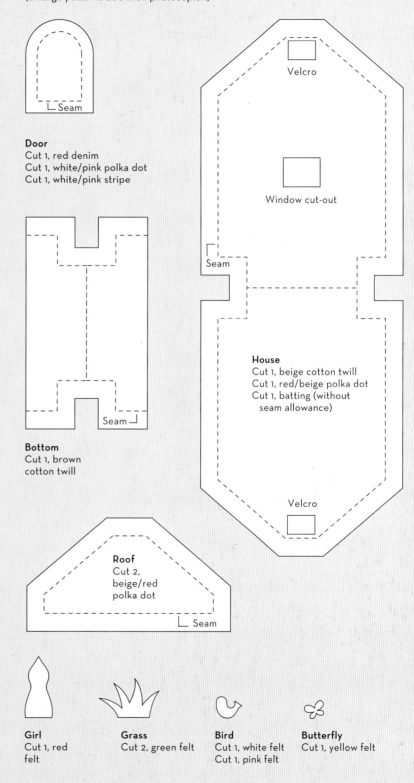

HOUSE CAMERA COZY PATTERNS
(Enlarge patterns 200% on photocopier.)

Door
Cut 1, red denim
Cut 1, white/pink polka dot
Cut 1, white/pink stripe

Bottom
Cut 1, brown cotton twill

Velcro

Window cut-out

Seam

House
Cut 1, beige cotton twill
Cut 1, red/beige polka dot
Cut 1, batting (without seam allowance)

Velcro

Roof
Cut 2, beige/red polka dot

Girl
Cut 1, red felt

Grass
Cut 2, green felt

Bird
Cut 1, white felt
Cut 1, pink felt

Butterfly
Cut 1, yellow felt

house
mug mat

Sip your hot chocolate in style
with your own handmade mug
mat. Stir, then tuck your spoon
into the mat's door-shaped
pocket, and enjoy!

Zakka Fact

In Japan, the tea ceremony
is an ancient tradition.
But nowadays the Japanese
also spend time in European-
style cafés and espresso
bars, which has led to the
development of *o-uchi café-style*,
or home café style, meaning
creating a café experience
at home by making cute
coasters and placemats for
your hot beverages.

Level of Difficulty

- -

Finished Size
6¼" x 7¼"

Materials
Fabric A: Scrap of linen, 12" x 10"
Fabric B: Scrap of cotton
   gingham, 8" x 10"
Fabric C: Scrap of printed cotton,
   4" square
Scrap of cotton batting, 12" x 10"
All-purpose thread to match linen
White glue
House Mug Mat pattern
   (see page 72)

Preparing the Fabric
CUT USING PATTERN
Fabric A: 1 house *(cut 4 square
   windows out of house)*;
   2 doors *(cut window out of
   1 door)*
Fabric B: 1 house
Cotton batting: 1 house, 1 door

CUT FREEHAND
Fabric C: 1 piece, 2¼" square
   *(for house windows back
   ground)*; 1 piece for door
   windows background *(use cut-
   out from door as guide and
   add ¼" all around)*; 1 circle,
   ⅜" in diameter *(for doorknob)*

- -

Seam Allowance
⅜"

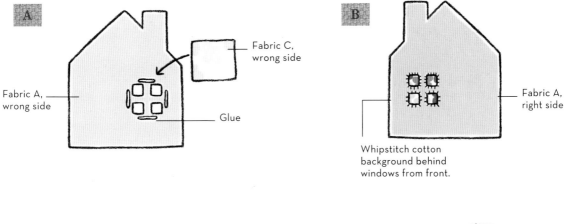

A

Fabric C,
wrong side

Fabric A,
wrong side

Glue

B

Fabric A,
right side

Whipstitch cotton
background behind
windows from front.

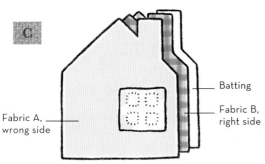

C

Batting

Fabric A,
wrong side

Fabric B,
right side

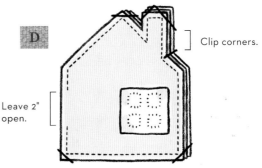

D

Clip corners.

Leave 2"
open.

1. Fill Background Behind Windows

Place the 2¼" square of Fabric C behind the linen house's cut-out windows. Use a tiny bit of glue around the edges of the cotton square to hold it in place *(Drawing A)*. Working from the right side of the linen house, sew the cotton background to the window cut-outs by whipstitching (see page 15) around each windowpane *(Drawing B)*.

2. Construct House

Stack the house's three layers, starting with the cotton batting. Then place and align the Fabric B house, right side up, on top of the batting and the Fabric A house, wrong side up, on top of the sandwich *(Drawing C)*. Stitch around the house sandwich with a ⅜" seam, leaving a 2" opening on one side *(Drawing D)*.

Clip the corners as shown, being careful not to clip into the stitched seam itself, and turn the house right side out. Sew the opening closed by hand.

3. Construct Door

Embellish the door: Place the Fabric C window background, wrong side up, on the wrong side of the linen door. Add a dab of glue around the edges of the window background to keep it in place *(Drawing E)*. Working on the linen's right side, use a dab of glue to position the door knob, as shown on the pattern, and whipstitch around both the window and the doorknob.

Construct the door: Stack and align the door pieces as follows: batting; linen door without a window, right side up; and linen door with the window, wrong side up. Stitch around the door's outer edge with a ³⁄₈" seam, leaving a 2" opening on one side. Trim the bottom corners, notch (see page 10) the top curved edge, and turn the door right side out through the opening. Sew the opening closed by hand.

4. Attach Door to House

Pin the door to the house, using the photograph on page 69 as a guide; hand-sew the sides and bottom of the door in place with a slipstitch (see page 15).

ZAKKA DESIGNER
fumi
www.lammymade.com

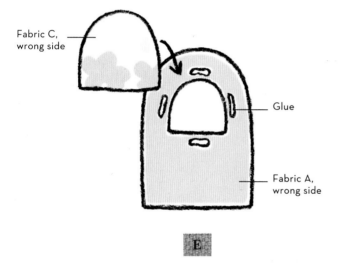

Fabric C, wrong side

Glue

Fabric A, wrong side

E

HOUSE MUG MAT PATTERN
(Enlarge patterns 200% on photocopier.)

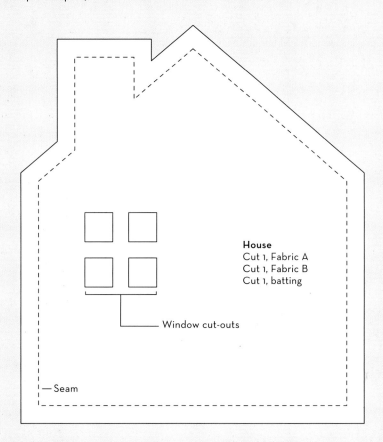

House
Cut 1, Fabric A
Cut 1, Fabric B
Cut 1, batting

Window cut-outs

— Seam

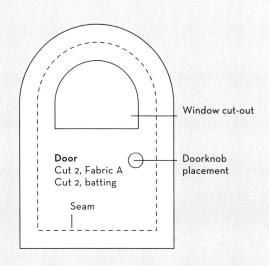

Window cut-out

Door
Cut 2, Fabric A
Cut 2, batting

Doorknob
placement

Seam

flower corsage
pincushion

Pretty wrist pincushions are the
perfect accessory for sewing—the
pins are always where you need
them. This one looks like a flower
corsage that you might have
worn to your high-school prom.
To change the size of the band,
measure your wrist and add 1"
plus an additional ½" for seam
allowances; this becomes your
strap measurement. All the other
measurements and directions
remain the same.

Zakka Fact

With so many people
crafting and sewing, making
a pincushion is a way to
demonstrate a personal style
with a practical object.
Tons of Made-in-Japan
pincushions were imported
to the United States in the
1940s – 1960s, including
the ever-popular tomato.

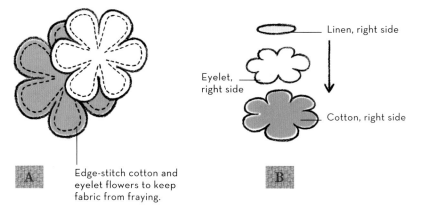

A

Edge-stitch cotton and eyelet flowers to keep fabric from fraying.

Linen, right side

Eyelet, right side

Cotton, right side

B

Level of Difficulty

- -

Finished Size

3" x 7¾"; strap, 1" wide

Materials

Scrap of linen, 6" x 8½"

Scrap of eyelet cotton, 4" square

Scrap of printed cotton, 4½" square

Scrap of tan wool felt, 1½" diameter circle

Plastic from gallon milk container, cut to 1⅜" diameter circle (for pincushion liner)

All-purpose thread to match fabrics

1" length of ⅝"-wide Velcro

Fiberfill

Flower pattern (on facing page)

Preparing the Fabric

CUT USING PATTERN

Cotton: 1 large flower

Eyelet cotton: 1 small flower

CUT FREEHAND

Linen: 1 circle, 1½" in diameter
    1 rectangle, 2½" x 8¼"

Wool felt: 1 circle, 1½" in diameter

Plastic: 1 circle, 1⅜" in diameter

- -

Seam allowance

¼"

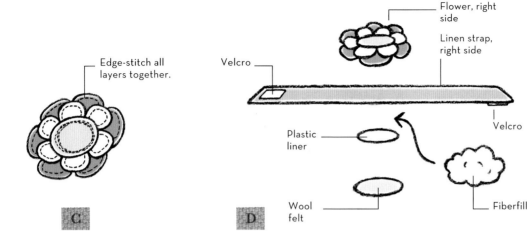

Edge-stitch all layers together.

C

Velcro

Flower, right side

Linen strap, right side

Velcro

Plastic liner

Wool felt

Fiberfill

D

1. Make Flower

Edge-stitch (see page 10) around the petals of both flowers, to deter fraying *(Drawing A)*.

Layer the flower pieces, right side up, from the bottom up as follows: large flower, small flower, and linen circle *(Drawing B)*. Adjust the two flowers so that their petals are "staggered" *(Drawing C)*, center the linen circle on the petals, and edge-stitch around the circle three times, sewing through all three layers. Set the flower aside.

2. Make Strap

Fold the linen rectangle in half lengthwise and press it. Then turn under the rectangle's three sides with raw edges by ¼" and press and pin these edges in place. Edge-stitch around all four sides.

Stitch the Velcro's loop side on one end of the strap and its hook side on the underside of the strap's other end *(Drawing D)*.

3. Put It All Together

Stack and pin the layers from the bottom up as follows: wool felt circle, plastic circle, strap, and flower *(Drawing D)*. Blanket-stitch (see page 12) the wool felt to the flower, leaving a 1" opening.

Stuff the circle with fiberfill, placing it between the plastic and strap. Hand-sew the opening closed.

Note

The fabric flowers' edges tend to fray; if you want a more finished look, use felt or Ultrasuede.

ZAKKA DESIGNER
anzu
http://ww8.tiki.ne.jp/~bruna/

FLOWER PATTERN
(Enlarge patterns 200% on photocopier.)

Large flower
Cut 1, cotton

Small flower
Cut 1, eyelet

flower
coasters

- - - - - - - - - - - - - - - - -

These beautiful felt coasters
are easy to make, and their
simple shapes will mix well
with other coaster designs
you create on your own,
such as leaves or fruit.

Zakka Fact

These simple motifs
resemble *wagashi*, traditional
Japanese sweets that are
often created with seasonal
themes. Flower-shaped
wagashi appear in stores in
Japan each spring.

Level of Difficulty

Finished Size
5" in diameter

Materials
Scraps of purple, lavender, and
    red felt, each cut to 6" x 11"
All-purpose thread in lavender,
    purple, red, and cream
Fabric scissors
White glue
Flower Coaster patterns
    (see facing page)

Preparing the Fabric
CUT USING PATTERNS
Lavender felt: 1 Flower A,
    1 Flower C
Purple felt: 1 Flower A, 1 Flower B
Red felt: 1 Flower B, 1 Flower C

Seam Allowance
None

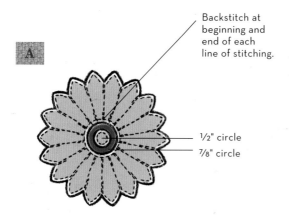

A

Backstitch at beginning and end of each line of stitching.

½" circle
⅞" circle

Flower A
Cut 1, lavender felt
Cut 1, purple felt

1. Make Flower A

Cut a ⅞"-diameter circle out of the center of the lavender Flower A. Trim the ⅞" circle so that it measures ½" in diameter and set it aside.

Using the cream thread in your machine, sew decorative stitching lines radiating out from the center to the edges of the petals, as indicated on the pattern. Backstitch (see page 11) at the beginning and end of each line of stitching (*Drawing A*).

Lightly glue the lavender flower on top of the same-shaped purple flower. Then pin and sew the pair together by edge-stitching (see page 10) around the center-circle opening with lavender thread.

Pin the ½" circle on the flower's center, and edge-stitch it to the flower with lavender thread. Finish the flower by edge-stitching around its outer edges with lavender thread.

2. Make Flower B

Cut a ½"-diameter circle out of the center of the purple Flower B.

Using cream thread in your machine, sew decorative lines from the cut-out center circle to the flower's petal edges, as shown on the pattern. Backstitch at the beginning and end of each line of stitching.

Lightly glue the purple flower to the red Flower B. Then pin and sew the pair together by edge-stitching around the circle with purple thread. Keeping the purple thread in the machine, edge-stitch around the petals' outer edges to finish the coaster.

3. Make Flower C

Using the red and lavender flowers, repeat the process in Step 2 for making Flower B, substituting red thread for purple thread.

ZAKKA DESIGNER
kabott
http://www.kabott.com

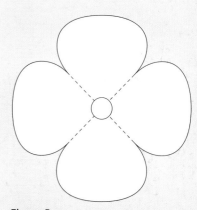

Flower B
Cut 1, purple felt
Cut 1, red felt

Flower C
Cut 1, red felt
Cut 1, lavender felt

bunny
pencil case

This cleverly designed pencil
case has ears that match its
lining, and the bunny's tail
becomes the zipper pull. Made
with a double layer of cotton
batting, this case will keep your
supplies safe and handy.

Zakka Fact

Move over Hello Kitty!
Cute bunnies—and pencil
cases to keep your pens
and pencils neatly stored—
are very popular in Japan.

Level of Difficulty

- -

Finished Size

4" x 9"

Materials

Linen, 12" square
Gingham, 12" square
Cotton batting, 12" square
7" zipper
4" length of linen/upholstery
    thread or hemp cord
    (for zipper pull)
All-purpose thread to
    match fabric
Fiberfill
White glue
Bunny Pencil Case pattern
    (see page 87)

Preparing the Fabric

NOTE: *The cutting and sewing
directions are for the linen bunny
with gingham ears.*

CUT USING PATTERNS
Linen: 2 bunnies, 2 ears
Gingham: 1 lining
    (cut on fold), 2 ears
Batting: 2 bunnies

CUT FREEHAND
Linen: 1 circle, 3" in
    diameter *(for tail)*

- -

Seam allowance

3/8"

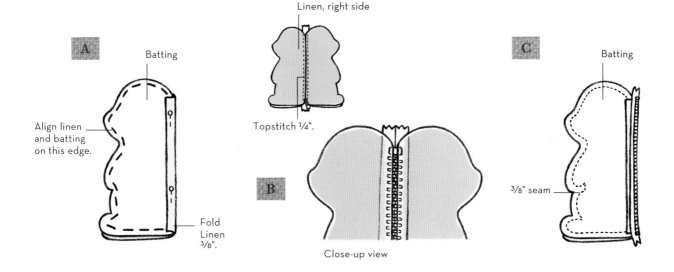

A
Batting
Align linen and batting on this edge.
Fold Linen ³⁄₈".

Linen, right side
Topstitch ¼".

B
Close-up view

C
Batting
³⁄₈" seam

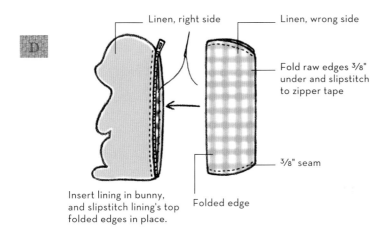

D
Linen, right side
Linen, wrong side
Fold raw edges ³⁄₈" under and slipstitch to zipper tape
³⁄₈" seam
Folded edge
Insert lining in bunny, and slipstitch lining's top folded edges in place.

1. Make Linen Bunny

With one linen bunny wrong side up, pin one batting bunny to the linen bunny, aligning the contoured edge (not the zipper edge), and baste (see page 9) the pair ¼" from the edge. Fold the zipper edge of the linen ³⁄₈" over the batting, and pin the fold in place *(Drawing A)*. Repeat the process with the other side of the bunny.

With the zipper zipped and its pull tab positioned at what will be the tail end of the bunny, pin one side of the zipper tape to the straight edge of one linen/batting bunny so that the folded edge of the linen sits in the center of the zipper teeth. Topstitch the zipper ¼" in from the folded edge and repeat the process with the other side of the bunny *(Drawing B)*.

With the fabrics' right sides together, pin the two bunny halves together. Join them with a ³⁄₈" seam *(Drawing C)*. Remove all the basting stitches.

Clip the inner curves and notch the outer curves (see page 10) around the bunny's body, making sure you don't cut into the seams. Turn the bunny right side out through the zipper.

2. Make and Attach Lining

Fold the lining in half lengthwise, with right sides together. Stitch along the lining's two short curved sides with a ³⁄₈" seam. With the lining still turned wrong side out, insert the lining into the bunny *(Drawing D)*. Turn under the lining's top edges ³⁄₈" and slipstitch (see page 15) these folded edges to the zipper tape on both sides.

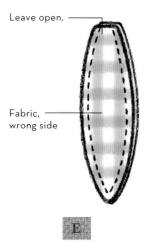

Leave open.

Fabric, wrong side

E

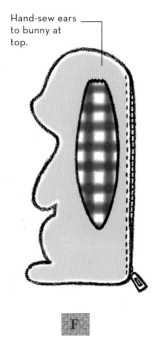

Hand-sew ears to bunny at top.

F

3. Make Bunny's Ears

With the fabrics' right sides together, pin one linen ear to one gingham ear. Join the two ears with a ³⁄₈" seam, leaving the straight edge at the top open *(Drawing E)*. Notch the ear's curves, and trim its point. Turn the ear right side out, and hand-sew it closed. Repeat the process to make the other ear.

4. Sew Ears to Bunny

Pin one ear to one side of the bunny's body, with the gingham side facing out *(Drawing F)*. Hand-stitch the ear's straight edge to attach it to the body. Repeat the process to attach the second ear.

5. Make Bunny's Tail

Make tail itself: Hand-sew a running stitch (see page 14) ³⁄₈" from the edge around the linen circle for the tail, leaving thread tails at the beginning and end of the stitching. Pull the thread tails gently to gather the circle into the beginning of a pouch. Stuff the pouch with fiberfill, and pull the thread tails snug to create a ball shape, but don't knot off the thread yet.

Make pull cord for tail: The designer crocheted a chain stitch in her hemp cording to make the pull cord to attach the bunny's tail to the zipper pull. An easy alternative is braiding three strands of heavy thread or embroidery floss. Make sure, though, that the braided cord is thin enough when folded in half to pass through the hole in the zipper pull.

Attach cord to zipper pull and tail: Fold the length of cord in half and insert the folded end through the hole in the zipper pull. Thread the two ends of the cord back through the loop that you've created, and pull the loop tight onto the zipper pull.

Dab a little glue on the cord's two ends, and insert these ends into the opening of the tail. Pull the gathering thread tight around the cord, tucking the raw edges of the linen inside the tail; hand-sew the tail's opening closed, taking a few stitches into the cord to secure it. Knot off the thread, and bury the thread tail in the bunny tail.

ZAKKA DESIGNER
fumi
www.lammymade.com

BUNNY PENCIL CASE PATTERNS
(Enlarge patterns 200% on photocopier.)

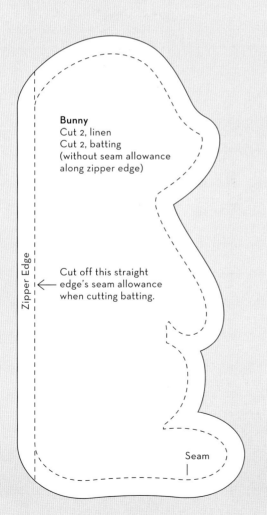

Bunny
Cut 2, linen
Cut 2, batting
(without seam allowance
along zipper edge)

Zipper Edge

Cut off this straight
edge's seam allowance
when cutting batting.

Seam

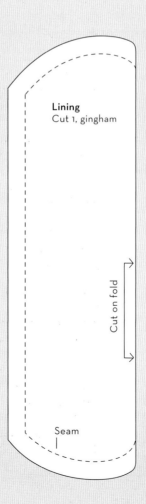

Lining
Cut 1, gingham

Cut on fold

Seam

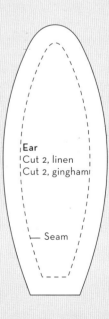

Ear
Cut 2, linen
Cut 2, gingham

Seam

sashiko
tea towel

- - - - - - - - - - - - - - - - - - -

Punch up a plain tea towel with
simple red sashiko embroidery.
The term *sashiko* literally
translates to "little stabs," and
this form of running stitches
has been used for centuries in
Japan to mend clothing and,
more recently, for decorative
quilting and embellishment.
There are dozens of Japanese
books with sashiko designs,
and this tea towel is a perfect
example of how to use a basic
one to enhance a simple object.

Zakka Fact

Is it any wonder that, in a
country with two thousand
years of tradition and
culture, sometimes old
techniques are rediscovered
by a new generation? Once
used by itinerant fishermen
as a way to repair and
reinforce their clothes, sashiko
embroidery is a good
example of *on ko chi shin*——
that is, taking a lesson from
the wisdom of the past.

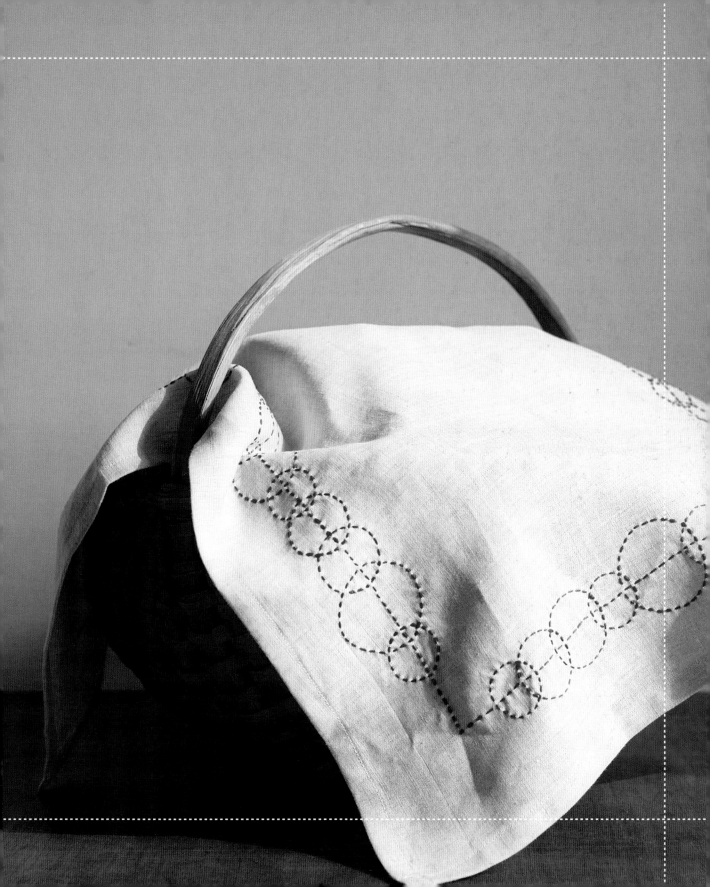

Level of Difficulty

Finished Size

17½" x 25"

Materials

Natural-color linen, 19½" x 27"

All-purpose thread to match linen

Red embroidery floss

Embroidery needle

5" length of linen ribbon tape
   (for hanging loop)

Water-soluble disappearing-ink pen

Sashiko template *(on facing page)*

Seam Allowance

1"

1. Hem Edges

With the linen laid flat, turn up the long edges ½", and press them in place; turn and press the edges again, ½" in the same direction, and pin the folded edges in place. Repeat the process with the linen's short edges. Edge-stitch (see page 10) both of the towel's short sides and one of its long sides, backstitching (see page 9) at the beginning and end of each line of stitching. *(Drawing A)*

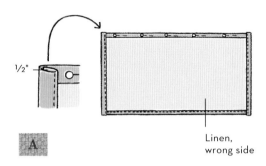

½"

A

Linen,
wrong side

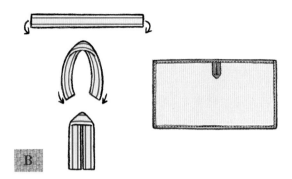

B

Fold the linen tape to make a loop, as shown in *Drawing B*. Insert the loop under the hem edge in the center of the towel's unsewn side, pin the loop in place, and iron it flat.

Edge-stitch this last side's hem, backstitching at the beginning and end of the seam.

2. Embroider Design
See page 14 for more on Sashiko stitching. Using the water-soluble disappearing-ink pen, transfer (see page 8) the sashiko template to all four edges of the tea towel's right side, positioning the design's straight, center line 2½" from the edge of each side. Note that on the towel's short edges, only about 8" of the 16" template will fit, so you'll be able to transfer only about eight of the circles along the straight center line. It's not important that the design on the short ends be symmetrical; in fact, varying the section of the template that you transfer gives the design variety and vitality. It is important, though, that you extend the straight center line out beyond each edge of the transferred design so that the center lines meet at each corner (see the photo on the facing page).

Using the red floss in your embroidery needle and bringing the floss up from the fabric's wrong side, embroider a Sashiko stitch (see page 14), following the lines of the transferred design. Neatly knot the floss on the towel's wrong side when you've completed the design or if you've finished a length of thread and need to start embroidering with a new length.

ZAKKA DESIGNER
Keiko Uemura
http://homepage2.nifty.com/gb_kei/

SASHIKO TEMPLATE
(Enlarge template 250% on photocopier.)

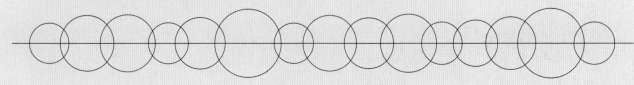

bird pot holder

Birds like this little sparrow are
a very popular motif in Japanese
zakka. Like the Appliqué Pot
Holder on page 18, this piece is
best used as a trivet for hot plates
or for handling pots on the
stovetop, not for taking very hot
pans out of the oven.

Zakka Fact

The sparrow is the most
common bird motif in
Japan. A famous Japanese
folktale called *Shitakiri
Suzume* (*The Tongue-Cut
Sparrow*) features this
sweet creature.

Level of Difficulty

- -

Finished Size

4½" x 10½"; leather loop, 7"

Materials

Scrap of linen, 13" x 14"

Scrap of printed cotton, 1" x 3"

Scrap of eyelet cotton, 3⅜" x 1"

Scrap of cotton lace, 4½" x ⅜"

Scrap of orange felt, 1½" x 3"

Scrap of thick cotton batting,
    13" x 14"

7½" length of ⅛"-wide
    leather cord

2 buttons, ¼" in diameter

All-purpose sewing thread
    to match linen

White glue

Bird Pot Holder pattern
    (see *facing page*)

Preparing the Fabric

CUT USING PATTERN

Linen: 2 birds

Cotton batting: 2 birds

CUT FREEHAND

Felt: 2 flowers or any shape
    you want

- -

Seam Allowance

⅜"

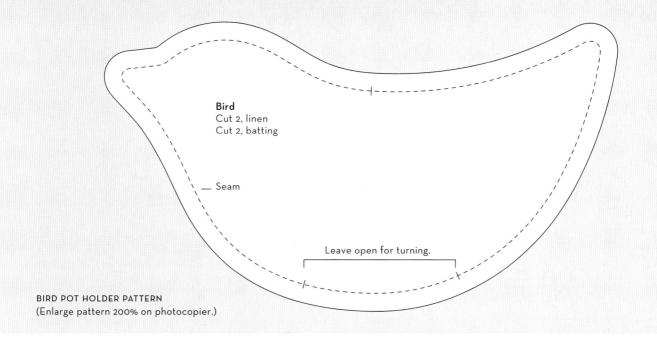

Bird
Cut 2, linen
Cut 2, batting

— Seam

Leave open for turning.

BIRD POT HOLDER PATTERN
(Enlarge pattern 200% on photocopier.)

1. Prepare Bird's Two Sides

To prepare the front, align and pin one cotton batting bird to one linen bird, and baste (see page 9) the two together.

Topstitch (see page 8) the trim to the linen bird, layering the trim as follows, from bottom to top: the eyelet, the printed cotton (turning the edges under ¼"), and the lace. Refer to the photographs for positioning the trim, or create your own design.

Lightly glue both felt flowers on top of the fabric/lace collage and sew the flowers in place stitching one button in the center of each flower.

To prepare the back, align and baste the second batting bird to the back of the second linen bird.

2. Sew Bird Together

With the linen right sides together, align and pin the bird front to the back *(Drawing A)*. Fold the leather cord in two, and insert the cord loop upside down between the front and back pieces.

Pin and stitch the layers together, leaving a 3" opening at the bottom of the bird *(Drawing B)*. Clip the inner curves and notch the outer curves (see page 10) on the bird's body. Trim the bird's beak and tail.

Turn the bird right side out through the opening and hand-sew the opening closed. Add a few decorative stitches near the collaged trim, if you want.

ZAKKA DESIGNER
Yukes
http://cozy-place.net/

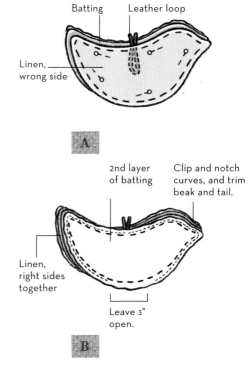

Batting   Leather loop

Linen,
wrong side

A

2nd layer   Clip and notch
of batting   curves, and trim
            beak and tail.

Linen,
right sides
together

Leave 3"
open.

B

balloon pouch

A whimsical design with a practical purpose, this pouch has a leather back (see page 98) that makes it substantial enough to hold your coins securely.

Zakka Fact

Children's illustrations and folktales often influence zakka designers in Japan. This charming little bag is totally *kawaii!*

Level of Difficulty

- -

Finished Size

4¼" x 5½"

- -

Materials

FABRIC
Scrap of cotton gingham, 5" x 5¼"
   (for outside front)
Scrap of linen, 6" x 8" (for back of
   outside front)
Scrap of cotton print, 12" x 6"
   (for lining)
Scrap of cotton batting, 6" x 12"

TRIM
Scraps of white felt and brown
   felt, each 3¾" x 1½"
11½" brown mini-rickrack,
   cut into two 5¾" lengths
2½" length of ½"-wide aqua
   scalloped ribbon

OTHER MATERIALS
Scrap of thin leather, 6" square
   (or substitute vinyl or felt,
   for balloon back)
Embroidery floss in brown, light
   blue, turquoise, and aqua
All-purpose thread to match
   linen, cotton lining, and zipper
   tape
Embroidery needle
6½" zipper
Fusible interfacing, 6" square
Water-soluble disappearing-ink
   pen
Balloon Pouch patterns
   (see page 101)

- -

Preparing the Fabric

CUT USING PATTERNS
Gingham: 1 balloon top *(use
   disappearing-ink pen to
   transfer zipper-placement
   marks to cut fabric's right side)*
Interfacing: 1 balloon top
Linen: 1 balloon body

Leather: 1 balloon body
   *(cut leather on pattern's
   seamline, not outer cutting
   line, since leather needs no
   seam allowance)*
Cotton print: 2 linings
   *(use disappearing-ink pen to
   transfer zipper-placement
   marks to cut fabric's right side)*
Cotton batting: 2 linings
White felt: 1 Cloud A, 1 Cloud B
Blue felt: 1 Bird A, 1 Bird B

CUT FREEHAND
Linen: 1 piece 2½" x 1¾"
   (for balloon basket)
Cotton batting: 2 circles,
   4" in diameter

- -

Seam allowance

⅜"

1. Embellish and Make Balloon Front

Embellish gingham balloon top: Lay the gingham balloon top right side up. Using two strands of turquoise floss in your embroidery needle and a running stitch (see page 14), hand-sew the brown rickrack to the balloon top (see *Drawing A* for placement). Set the balloon top aside.

Embellish linen balloon basket: With the linen basket right side up, lay the ribbon, right side up, across its top edge. Machine-baste (see page 9) across the ribbon, ¼" below its top edge *(Drawing B)*.

Join balloon basket and gingham top: With the fabrics' right sides together, align and pin the linen basket at the bottom edge of the gingham balloon top *(Drawing C)*. Using all-purpose thread to match the lining, stitch the pair together with a ⅜" seam along their pinned straight edge. Flip the basket piece down, so its right side shows and press the balloon top/basket flat.

Interface balloon top: Apply the fusible interfacing to the wrong side of the gingham balloon top, following the interfacing manufacturer's directions for correct iron setting and application.

Join balloon front and "liner": With the fabrics' right sides together, align and pin the linen balloon body to the gingham balloon-body front, and sew around the perimeter of the pair with a ⅜" seam, leaving the bottom edge of the basket open *(Drawing D)*. Turn the balloon right side out through the opening, fold up the seam allowances on the balloon basket, and hand-sew the basket's opening closed.

Embellish balloon front: Using a single strand of the aqua floss and a blanket stitch (see page 12), hand-sew both clouds on the front of the balloon (see the pattern on page 101 for placing for this and the next embellishment of birds). Using a single strand of light blue floss and a blanket stitch, hand-sew both birds on the front of the balloon.

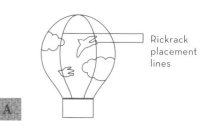

Rickrack placement lines

A

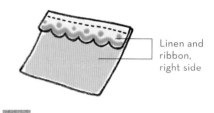

Linen and ribbon, right side

B

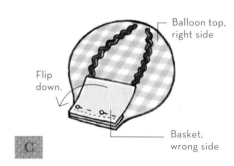

Balloon top, right side

Flip down.

Basket, wrong side

C

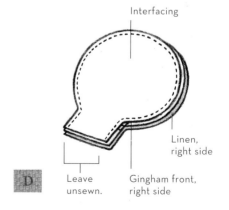

Interfacing

Linen, right side

Leave unsewn.

Gingham front, right side

D

2. Sew Balloon Front to Back

Lay the fabric balloon front right side down and position the leather balloon back right side up on top, aligning their edges (the wrong sides of the front and back will be facing one another). Hand-sew the front and back together, using a running stitch (see page 14) and two strands of brown floss and leaving unsewn the space between the zipper markings you transferred from the pattern to the gingham fabric *(Drawing E)*. If you start stitching on the left side of the zipper opening, with the leather back face up, and stitch around the bottom of the pouch to the other side of the zipper opening, you can just leave the needle and floss hanging until you position the zipper in the next step to sew it in place. Sewing in this way will also enable you to finish up the next step so that you can knot off the thread on the front pouch's fabric liner.

3. Attach Zipper

With the balloon still turned right side out, pin the zipper tape in place along the inside edges of the opening of the balloon front and back. With the pouch's leather back face up, pick up the floss and needle that you were sewing with in the previous step and sew the zipper tape in place on the pouch back's opening edge, continuing the running stitches you used to sew the front and back of the pouch together *(Drawing F)*. When you get to the end of the zipper opening on the back, insert the needle and

pull it through to the front of the pouch. Then stitch the zipper tape along the front's opening edge with the same running stitches. When you've finished stitching the zipper tape, pull your needle and thread through to the inside of the pouch and knot off on the front's fabric liner.

4. Make Lining for Pouch

Baste a circle of cotton batting to the wrong side of each cotton-print lining piece. With the fabrics' right sides together, pin the two basted linings together. Stitch around the lining circle with a ³/₈" seam, leaving unsewn the opening you marked for the zipper on the cotton-print linings. Notch the curves (see page 10) and press the fabric flat around the batting *(Drawing G)*.

5. Finish Pouch

Insert the lining unit inside the pouch (the batting sides of the lining will face the wrong sides of the balloon) *(Drawing H)*. Using thread the color of your zipper tape, hand-sew the lining to the zipper tape with a slipstitch (see page 15) *(Drawing I)*.

ZAKKA DESIGNER
moko moko
http://www.niji.or.jp/home/
mokomoko2/

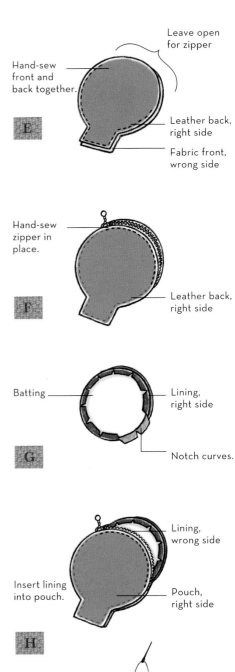

Leave open for zipper

Hand-sew front and back together.

E

Leather back, right side

Fabric front, wrong side

Hand-sew zipper in place.

F

Leather back, right side

Batting

G

Lining, right side

Notch curves.

Lining, wrong side

Insert lining into pouch.

Pouch, right side

H

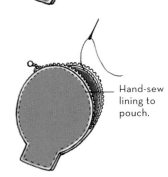

Hand-sew lining to pouch.

I

BALLOON POUCH PATTERNS
(Enlarge patterns 200% on photocopier.)

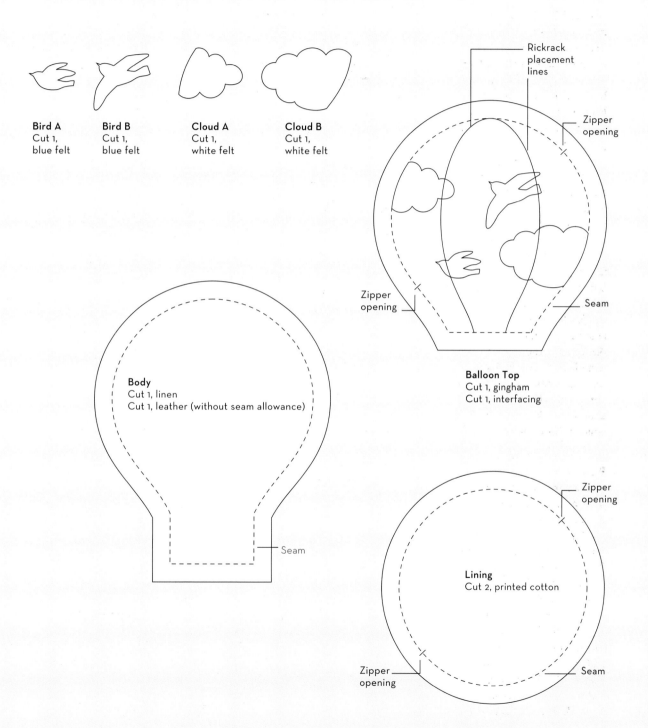

Bird A
Cut 1,
blue felt

Bird B
Cut 1,
blue felt

Cloud A
Cut 1,
white felt

Cloud B
Cut 1,
white felt

Rickrack placement lines

Zipper opening

Zipper opening

Seam

Balloon Top
Cut 1, gingham
Cut 1, interfacing

Body
Cut 1, linen
Cut 1, leather (without seam allowance)

Seam

Zipper opening

Lining
Cut 2, printed cotton

Zipper opening

Seam

sashiko
placemats

The black-and-white design
of these placemats is
modern and sophisticated—
and then softened with
the traditional sashiko
embroidery in muted colors.

Zakka Fact

This sashiko design is called
karakusa—a Chinese pattern
with a repeating motif of
scrolling vines and tendrils.
The design was first
introduced to Japan in the
8th century, but it wasn't
until the 17th century that
it began to be used to
decorate a wide variety of
fabrics, including those used
for futon covers and *furoshiki*,
or wrapping cloths.

Level of Difficulty

FinishedSize
12½" x 17"

Materials

NOTE: *Directions are for the placemat with sashiko embroidery on lower black panel.*

Scrap of black linen, 6" x 18" *(for embroidered panel)*
Scrap of white linen, 22" x 18", cut into 1 piece, 8½" x 19", and 1 piece, 13½" x 18" *(for lower panel and back of placemat)*
Embroidery floss in white, black, and yellow
All-purpose thread in black and white
Embroidery needle
Water-soluble disappearing-ink pen
Sashiko Template
(see facing page)

Seam Allowance
½"

1. Make and Embellish Front Panel

Align and pin the lower edge of the upper (wider) white panel to the upper edge of the lower (narrower) black panel (the pair of placemats shown above alternates black and white linen on top and bottom). Using all-purpose black thread in your machine, stitch the pair together along the long side with a ½" seam. Press the seam open.

Prepare for embellishing the black panel by transferring (see page 8) the sashiko template at right onto the black panel with the disappearing-ink pen. Then, following the transferred pattern lines, alternately use the white and yellow floss to hand-embroider the lines with a sashiko stitch (see page 14). (For the other placemat with the white lower panel, use black and olive floss alternately to embroider the design.) There's really no right or wrong way to combine the two colors in this piece. Just make sure the combination you choose pleases *your* eye. Then, using black floss (or white floss for the other placemat), hand-embroider a large running stitch across the lower edge of the placemat's upper panel, 1/4" above from the seam.

2. Join Front and Back Panels

With the fabrics' right sides together, align and pin the front panel to the white back panel; and join the pair, stitching along all four sides with a 1/2" seam. Leave a 4" opening on one side for turning.

Trim the placemat's corners, turn it right side out, and press it flat with a hot iron from the wrong side—do not iron directly on top of the sashiko embroidery.

3. Edge-Stitch Placemat

To finish the placemat, edge-stitch around it entirely, working from the right side, sewing 1/16" from the edge, and switching thread in your machine as follows: Use black thread as the top thread when edge-stitching the black panel and switch to white thread when edge-stitching the white panel. Keep white thread in the bobbin throughout, however, so the bobbin thread on the back of the placemat will match the placemat's white linen back. Be sure to backstitch (see page 11) at the beginning and end of your edge-stitching before changing the thread.

ZAKKA DESIGNER
Keiko Uemura
http://homepage2.nifty.com/ gb_kei/

STITCHING TEMPLATE
(Enlarge template 250% on photocopier.)

bunny wallet

Whether you're carrying dollars, euros, or yen, this adorable bunny wallet will keep your cash and credit cards safe.

Zakka Fact

Rabbits are a part of many popular mythologies in Japan. For instance, Japanese believe that there is a rabbit on the moon—not a man in the moon as in Western cultures. This rabbit is supposed to be making rice cakes, which are traditionally eaten to celebrate Jugoya, the day of the first autumn moon.

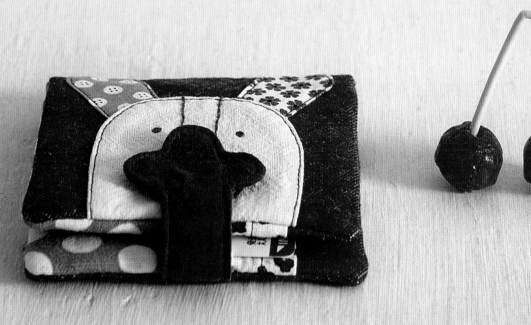

Level of Difficulty

Finished Size

4" square

Materials

FABRIC

Fabric A: Scrap of red denim,
  2 pieces, 8½" x 4¾"
  (for wallet body)

Fabric B: Scrap of black-polka-
  dotted white linen, 4¾" x 6¼"
  (for coin pocket)

Fabric C: Scrap of red-flower-
  print cotton, 4⅛" x 8½"
  (for bill pocket)

Fabric D: Scrap of white-polka-
  dotted green cotton, 3⅜" x
  8½" *(for credit-card pockets)*

Fabric E: Scrap of tan cotton,
  3" x 3¼" *(for face)*

Fabric F: Scrap of green button
  print cotton, 2¾" x 1½" *(for
  ear)*

Fabric G: Scrap of red daisy
  cotton, 2¾" x 1½" *(for 2nd ear)*

Fabric H: Scrap of red-striped
  ticking, 1½" x 2"
  (for coin-pocket pull-tab)

Fabric I: Scrap of brown cotton,
  2" x 3⅛" *(for paw snap-closure)*

OTHER MATERIALS

Fusible interfacing, 2 pieces,
  8½" x 4¾"

Extra-thin cotton batting, 2" x 3⅛"

Purple embroidery floss

All-purpose red sewing thread
  *(use for both construction and
  all edge- and topstitching)*

3½" length of ½"-wide Velcro

½"-diameter snap

Bunny Wallet pattern
  (see page 11)

Preparing the Fabric

CUT USING PATTERNS

Fabric E: 1 bunny face

Fabric F: 1 ear

Fabric G: 1 ear (cut in reverse)

Fabric I: 2 paws

Cotton batting: 1 paw

Seam Allowance

⅜"

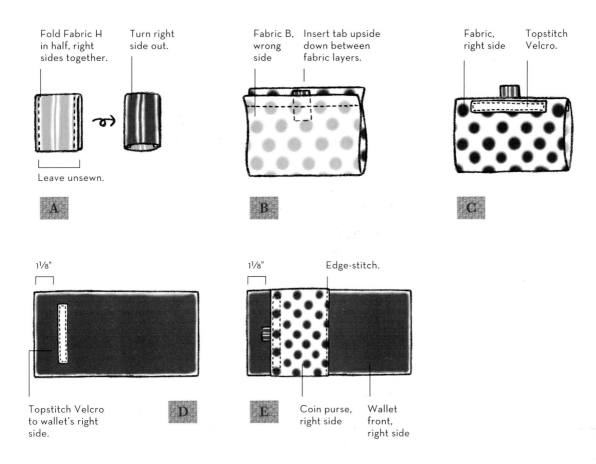

Fold Fabric H in half, right sides together.

Turn right side out.

Leave unsewn.

A

Fabric B, wrong side

Insert tab upside down between fabric layers.

B

Fabric, right side

Topstitch Velcro.

C

1⅛"

Topstitch Velcro to wallet's right side.

D

1⅛"

Edge-stitch.

E

Coin purse, right side

Wallet front, right side

1. Make Coin Pocket

Make pull-tab: With the right sides together, fold the Fabric H pull-tab in half, matching up the short sides. With red thread in your machine, sew the long sides together with a ⅜" seam, leaving the bottom edge unsewn *(Drawing A).* Turn the pull-tab right side out through the opening, and iron it flat.

Make coin pocket: With the fabric's right sides together, fold Fabric B in half, matching up and pinning the short sides.

Insert the pull-tab upside down and centered between the right sides of folded fabric, making sure the unsewn edge of the pull-tab is aligned with the unsewn edges of the folded fabric *(Drawing B).*

Stitch across the top of the coin pocket with a ⅜" seam, and turn the pocket right side out through one open side. Pin one half of the Velcro at top on the underside of the coin pocket, and topstitch the Velcro in place from the pocket's right side *(Drawing C).* Sew the corresponding Velcro

half to the red denim wallet front, positioning it 1⅛" from the raw edge *(Drawing D).*

Pin the coin pocket to the wallet front 1⅛" away from the edge, and edge-stitch (see page 10) the bottom edge of the coin pocket *(Drawing E).* Then, with the wallet front wrong side up, position and apply the interfacing, resin side down, on the wallet front according to the manufacturer's instructions.

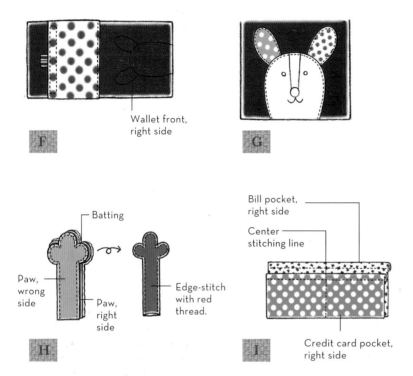

Wallet front,
right side

F

G

─ Batting

Paw,
wrong
side

Paw,
right
side

Edge-stitch
with red
thread.

H

Bill pocket,
right side

Center
stitching line

Credit card pocket,
right side

I

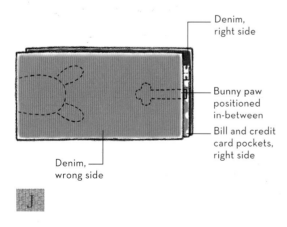

Denim,
right side

Bunny paw
positioned
in-between

Bill and credit
card pockets,
right side

Denim,
wrong side

J

2. Create Bunny's Face

Attach the ears: Clip along the curve (see page 10) on each cotton-print bunny ear and the tan cotton face, being careful to make clips no deeper than ⅛". With each ear wrong side up, turn under the edges all around each ear ¼", and press. Pin both ears to the wallet front (see *Drawing F* for placement, and note that the ears are set at a slight angle to the head). Edge-stitch around each ear.

Attach the face: With the bunny face wrong side up, turn and press the fabric's edge ¼" all around to the wrong side. Pin the bunny face on the wallet front so that it overlaps the bottom edge of the ears. Edge-stitch around the face.

Add the nose and other features: Using a single strand of purple floss in your embroidery needle, hand-sew the snap in the area of the bunny's nose, 1" from the fabric's bottom raw edge and centered between the two side edges. Then, using a doubled strand of the purple floss, hand-embroider the bunny's nose and mouth with a backstitch (see page 11), make eyes with a French knot or a satin stitch (see pages 13 or 15), and set the wallet front aside *(Drawing G).*

BUNNY WALLET PATTERN
(Enlarge patterns 200% on photocopier.)

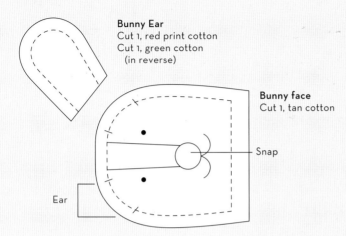

Bunny Ear
Cut 1, red print cotton
Cut 1, green cotton
  (in reverse)

Bunny face
Cut 1, tan cotton

— Snap

Ear

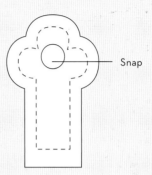

Bunny Paw
Cut 2, brown cotton
Cut 1, batting

— Snap

3. Make Bunny's Paw

With right sides together, align the two Fabric I bunny paws. Then align the batting paw on one side of the fabric paws, and pin all three layers together. Stitch around the paw with a ¼" seam, leaving the short end open. Notch the curves (see page 10), trim the corners, turn the paw right side out through the opening, and edge-stitch around the paw *(Drawing H)*.

4. Make Interior Wallet Sections

Make bill pocket: Turn Fabric C wrong side up, and turn and press one long edge ⅜" to the wrong side; then turn and press this edge again, ⅜" to the wrong side. Topstitch the folded edge along the upper fold *(Drawing I)*.

Make credit-card pocket: Repeat the process above to turn the edge of Fabric D, which will hold credit cards. Align and pin this pocket, right side up, on top of the red floral-print bill pocket, also right side up, matching up their bottom edges. Stitch a line down the center of the green pocket, backstitching (see page 9) at the beginning and end of the seam to create the pockets for credit cards *(Drawing I)*.

5. Sew It All Together

Stack the wallet parts as follows, from the bottom up *(Drawing J)*: red denim wallet piece (without the bunny appliqué), right side up; red floral print/green polka-dotted piece, wrong side up, with the bottom edge aligned with the bottom edge of the red denim; the bunny's paw inserted at the center right edge; and the red denim wallet front with the appliqué, wrong side up.

Stitch around the wallet's edges with a ⅜" seam, leaving a 2" opening on one side. Trim the corners, turn the wallet right side out through the opening, and hand-sew the opening closed. Press the wallet. Using a strand of purple floss, hand-sew the matching snap half in place on the inside of the bunny's paw.

ZAKKA DESIGNER
kazu
http://www18.ocn.ne.jp/~fabric-k/

merci apron

- -

This apron is beautifully
made with vintage handspun
linen in the center panel and
lots of extra finishing details
throughout. Each apron string
is made with eight different
fabrics and embellished with an
embroidered running stitch to
unify the design.

Zakka Fact

This piece melds several
Japanese trends—linen for
a rustic look, a foreign word
used as a design element,
and sashiko embroidery that
adds color and texture.
(For more on the history of
sashiko, see page 88).

Level of Difficulty

- -

Finished Size

19¼" x 36"; apron strings, 1" x 32" each

Materials

FABRIC

Natural-color linen, 17¼" x 21¾" *(for center panel)*

White linen. 21½" x 23" *(for side panels)*

Brown gingham, two strips, each 1½" x 32½" *(for back of apron strings)*

8–12 scraps of printed or variously woven linen and/or cotton to make 3" x 32½" patchwork *(to be cut into two strips, each 1½" x 32½", for front of apron strings)*

TRIM

Scrap of linen, about 1⅜" x 4¼"

Scrap of linen, about 2½" x 3½"

Scrap of linen, about 1⅞" x 3¼"

Scrap of lace, about 2" x 3"

Scrap of lace, about 3½" by 2"

Embroidery floss in red, blue, fuchsia, brown, green, and purple

OTHER MATERIALS

Water-soluble disappearing-ink pen

All-purpose off white thread

Embroidery needle

Merci lettering template (see page 117)

- -

Seam Allowance

⅝" for apron; ¼" for apron strings

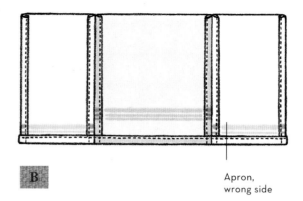

A

B

Apron,
wrong side

1. Embroider and Apply Appliqués to Apron Front

Use the template provided on page 117 and a disappearing-ink pen to transfer the *Merci* lettering to the center of the center linen panel.

Lay the linen and lace trim appliqués around the transferred lettering, making sure a couple of appliqués overlap several letters (see photograph on page 113). Zigzag-stitch the appliqués in place using off-white thread.

Use the disappearing-ink pen to redraw the parts of the letters covered up by the appliqués so that you'll maintain the outline of the letters.

Fill in the letters with a series of sashiko stitches (see page 114), as shown in *Drawing A*. Use blue floss in your embroidery needle to stitch the *M*, fuchsia for the *e*, brown for the *r*, green for the *c*, and purple for the *i*—or any color combination you prefer.

2. Sew Apron Panels Together

With right sides together, pin the apron's side panels to the center panel, and stitch each pair of panels together with a ⁵⁄₈" seam. Press the seams open, fold under each seam allowance ¼" to the wrong side, and pin the fold in place. Working from the apron's wrong side, edge-stitch (see page 10) each seam allowance's folded edge *(Drawing B)*.

Hem the apron's side edges by turning each edge under ¼" to the wrong side and pressing it in place, then turning and pressing it again by ⅜". Pin and edge-stitch the hem on each side.

To hem the bottom edge, fold the fabric by ¼" to the wrong side and press it in place; then fold and press it again by ⅜". Topstitch the double-folded edge along the upper fold.

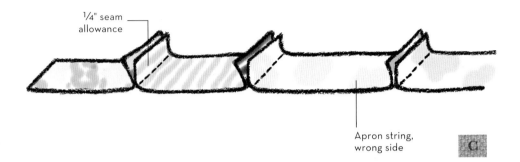

¼" seam allowance

Apron string, wrong side

C

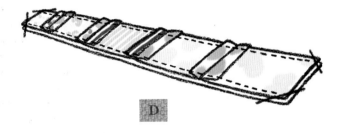

D

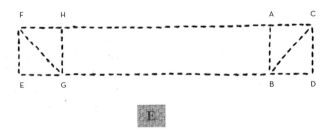

F   H   A   C

E   G   B   D

E

3. Make Apron Strings

Arrange the patchwork pieces for the front of the apron string in any order you like. Starting at one end of the apron string, lay the first piece on top of the second piece, with right sides together, and sew the short ends with a $1/4$" seam *(Drawing C)*. Repeat this step to attach each new fabric to the patchwork string until it's approximately $32^1/2$" long. Press all the seams open, and cut the patchwork in half along its length, so you have two strips $1^1/2$" x $32^1/2$".

Align one patchwork strip on top of one brown gingham strip, with right sides together. Sew both long sides, but leave the short sides unsewn. Trim the corners *(Drawing D)*.

Turn the apron string right side out. (It's helpful to attach a safety pin to one short end of the strip, push the pin in the strip, and work it through the strip's length to turn the fabric right side out). Then fold in the seam allowances $1/4$" on one short end, press them, and hand-sew the opening closed. (You can leave the other short end as is, since it will be covered when you attach the string to the apron in the next step.) Press the apron string with a hot iron.

Using two strands of red floss, hand-embroider a running stitch (see page 14) $1/8$" in from the edge along one long side of the string, across the short, finished edge, and back down the other long side.

Repeat this step to make the second apron string.

4. Attach Apron Strings

Fold and press the top edge of the apron $1/2$" to the wrong side. Fold and press this edge again, $1^1/4$" to the wrong side. Insert 1" of the raw end of one apron string into the waistband fold, making sure the apron string's patchwork side faces the same direction as the apron's right side; pin the apron string in place. Repeat this step with the other apron string.

Topstitch the waistband and end of the apron strings, as shown in *Drawing E*, starting at Point A and proceeding to Point B, Point C, and so on through point H. Backstitch (see page 11) at Point A and Point H. Then start stitching again at Point F, and stitch across to Point C, again backstitching at Point F and Point C.

ZAKKA DESIGNER
kazu
http://www18.ocn.ne.jp/~fabric-k/

room shoes

Toss the flip-flops and settle in at home with these pretty slippers, called "room shoes" in Japan. They're made with linen, cotton batting, and a little bit of elastic for a snug fit. This is a challenging sewing project, but once you've made these shoes and put them on, you won't want to take them off!

Zakka Fact

In Japan, when you enter a home, it's customary to leave your shoes at the door and put on slippers. These sweet room shoes are padded for comfort and have a leather sole. They are a very feminine version of the traditional slip-on footwear that both men and women traditionally wear in Japanese homes.

Level of Difficulty

Finished Size
Approximate American size 7
  (see information on
  changing shoe size at
  end of project)

Materials
Linen, 13" x 19"

Cotton gingham, 13" x 27½"

Lightweight tan leather, 11" x 9"

Embroidery floss in purple,
  lavender, brown, green,
  and beige

8" length of ½"-wide elastic, cut
  into two 4" lengths

Quilting or upholstery thread
  (for sewing leather soles)

All-purpose thread to match linen

Fusible interfacing

Embroidery needle

Water-soluble disappearing-ink pen

Room Shoes pattern
  (see page 125)

Preparing the Fabric
The Room Shoes patterns are for
the left foot. To make a pair of
shoes, cut the number of pieces
noted on the pattern and turn
half of them over so that you'll
have mirror-image piece(s) for
the right foot (since linen and
gingham are the same on both
sides, turning the cut pattern over
poses no problem). To prevent any
confusion as you work, divide the
cut pieces into separate stacks
for the left and right foot, and
mark the wrong side of all the cut
pieces with a disappearing-ink
pen. Note that the pattern pieces
have a built-in ⅜" seam allowance and also that you need to
use the disappearing-ink pen to
transfer to the wrong side of the
cut pieces the pattern's strap-
placement marks and the marked
Points A–E.

CUT USING PATTERNS

Linen: 2 shoe bodies

Gingham: 2 shoe bodies, 2 soles

Leather: 2 soles

Cotton batting: 2 shoe bodies,
  4 soles (cut without seam
  allowances)

Interfacing: 2 shoe bodies

CUT FREEHAND

Linen: 2 pieces, 5¼" x 2¼"
  (for straps; note that piece has
  built-in ½" seam allowance)

Seam Allowance
⅜"

1. Make Straps

Fold one linen rectangle in half lengthwise. Using all-purpose thread in your machine, sew the rectangle's long sides together with a ⅜" seam. Turn the strap right side out, centering the seam on what will be the underside of the strap. Insert the elastic in the strap and baste (see page 9) it to each end, bunching up the linen over the elastic *(Drawing A)*.

Repeat to make the second strap, and set both straps aside.

2. Embellish Linen Shoe Body

Using the Blueberries Template on page 124, transfer (see page 8) the image to the toe of each linen shoe body (see the photo on the facing page for placement).

Use a satin stitch (see page 15) and your embroidery needle to hand-embroider the two blueberries on the stem with purple floss and the floating berry with lavender floss. Add a few straight running stitches (see page 14) on top of or next to one another in beige floss to decorate each berry. Embroider the leaves with green floss and a fishbone stitch (see page 13) or a standard satin stitch. Create the stem with brown floss and a satin stitch.

3. Make Shoe Body

Interface linen shoe body: With one linen shoe body wrong side up, align the corresponding interfacing piece, resin side down, on top of the shoe body and iron the interfacing according to the manufacturer's instructions to attach it.

Notch toe and sew gathering stitches: Notch the curve (see page 10) around the toe. With the all-purpose thread still in your machine, sew two rows of gathering stitches (see page 14) around the toe from Point B to D, being careful to stitch *inside* the ⅜" seam allowance and leaving thread tails on each end of the stitching line *(Drawing B)*.

Sew heel seam: Align the heels of the shoe body, with the right sides together, and sew the heel with a ⅜" seam. Press the seam open *(Drawing C)*.

Adjust gathering stitches to match sole: Pull the thread tails on both ends of the two rows of gathering stitches to gather up the toe so that Points B and D on the shoe body match up with Points B and D on the sole *(Drawing C)*, distributing the gathers evenly between Points B and D. Secure the gathered stitches on the toe with a knot at each end.

Repeat the entire process to make the second shoe.

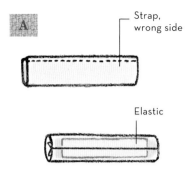

A

Strap, wrong side

Elastic

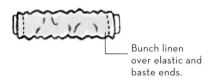

Strap, right side, with seam centered and elastic inserted

Bunch linen over elastic and baste ends.

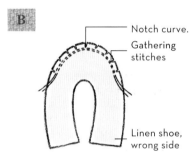

B

Notch curve.

Gathering stitches

Linen shoe, wrong side

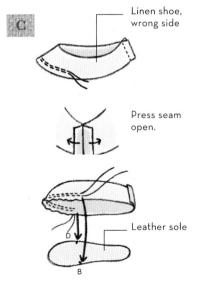

C

Linen shoe, wrong side

Press seam open.

Leather sole

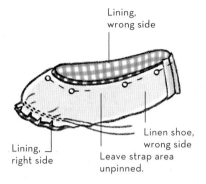

Lining, wrong side

Linen shoe, wrong side

Lining, right side

Leave strap area unpinned.

Leave open for strap.

Stitch top edge.

Clip inner curve.

Linen shoe, wrong side

Lining, right side

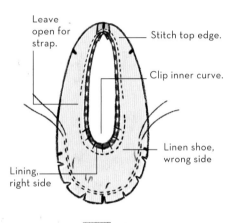

Lining, right side

Edge-stitch.

Stitch second row to reinforce strap.

Linen shoe, right side

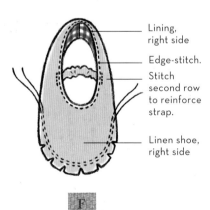

4. Make Body Lining

Baste one cut batting body to the wrong side of one gingham body lining. With the lining's right sides together and the heels aligned, sew the heel with a ³⁄₈" seam.

Gather the toe area, as you did with the linen shoe body in Step 3, again matching up Points B and D with the same points on the leather sole. Repeat the process with the second gingham body lining.

5. Attach Body to Lining

Align the linen shoe body and lining, with right sides together. Pin around the inner edge where your foot slides into the shoe, leaving unpinned the two strap-placement spots you marked for later inserting the ends of the strap *(Drawing D)*.

Stitch the pinned inner edge with a ³⁄₈" seam. Clip around the curve on the inner edge, being careful not to cut into the seam itself *(Drawing E)*.

Turn the shoe right side out and insert the strap on each side. Edge-stitch around the entire inner edge ¹⁄₈" from the edge to finish it and attach the strap. To reinforce the strap, add a second row of stitching on each side of the strap that's ⁵⁄₈" long and ¹⁄₄" down from the edge. Backstitch at the beginning and end of your stitching *(Drawing F)*.

Repeat the process above for the second shoe, and set shoes aside.

6. Make Leather Sole

Align and center two cut batting soles on the wrong side of one leather sole. Using quilting or upholstery thread in your machine, baste around the edge of the batting layers to attach them to the sole *(Drawing G)*.

To quilt the layers together, work on the right side of the sole and sew five ³⁄₄"-wide star shapes by overlapping several short rows of straight stitches, backstitching each end to reinforce it (see the photo on page 120 for placement).

Repeat the process for the second sole.

7. Sew Leather Sole to Linen Body

Pin the leather sole to the linen body, with right sides together, matching Points A, B, and D. Adjust the gathering stitches as needed so that the two pieces fit together smoothly. Pin around the rest of the shoe, attaching the linen body to the sole and matching the remaining Points C and E. The linen body's heel seam should match the notch at the heel of the leather sole *(Drawing H)*. Stitch the sole to the linen body with a ³⁄₈" seam *(Drawing I)*.

Repeat the process to make the second shoe.

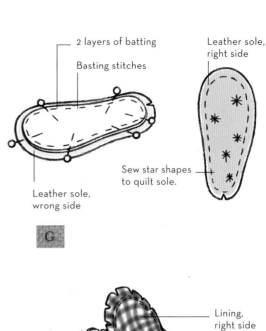

2 layers of batting

Basting stitches

Leather sole, right side

Leather sole, wrong side

Sew star shapes to quilt sole.

G

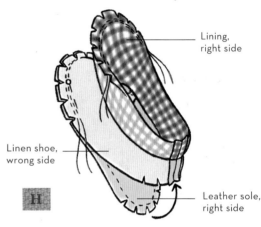

Lining, right side

Linen shoe, wrong side

Leather sole, right side

H

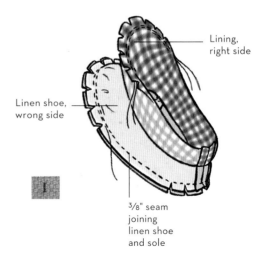

Lining, right side

Linen shoe, wrong side

³⁄₈" seam joining linen shoe and sole

I

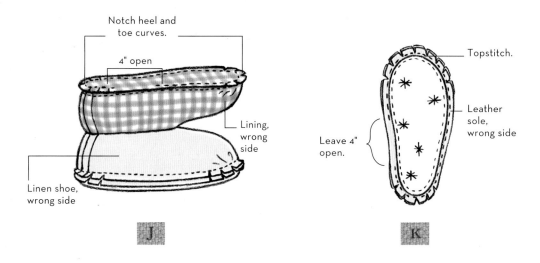

Notch heel and toe curves.

4" open

Lining, wrong side

Linen shoe, wrong side

J

Topstitch.

Leather sole, wrong side

Leave 4" open.

K

8. Attach Gingham Lining Sole to Gingham Lining Body

Pin and topstitch the gingham sole to the gingham lining body (as in Step 7) with a ⅜" seam allowance, matching the corresponding points and leaving a 4" opening on one side. Notch the toe and heel curves *(Drawing J)*.

To reinforce all the layers, pull the gingham lining down over the linen shoe, and topstitch around the outer edge inside the seam allowance, leaving unstitched the existing 4" opening for turning *(Drawing K)*. Turn the shoe right side out through the opening and sew the opening closed by hand.

Repeat the process on the second shoe.

Note:
Adjusting Shoe Size

These slippers will accommodate approximately a 6½ to 8 shoe size. If you want to adjust the pattern for a larger or smaller shoe size, here's how: Start by enlarging or reducing the sole pattern for the batting (that is, the sole pattern minus the seam allowance) to match your foot. To do this, first place your foot on a piece of paper, draw an outline around it, and compare your outline to the batting sole pattern. Enlarge or reduce the batting sole pattern on a copy machine until it matches the outline of your foot, and note the percentage on the copy machine at which you enlarged or reduced the pattern.

Next cut out the shoe body pattern along the seam line (not the outer-edge cutting line). Then enlarge or reduce this pattern on the copy machine by the same amount you enlarged or reduced the batting sole pattern. Finally, add a ⅜" seam allowance around the entire edge of both newly sized patterns, and cut them out.

ZAKKA DESIGNER
sachiko nakano
http://safran-seed.com

ROOM SHOES PATTERN
(Enlarge patterns 200% on photocopier.)

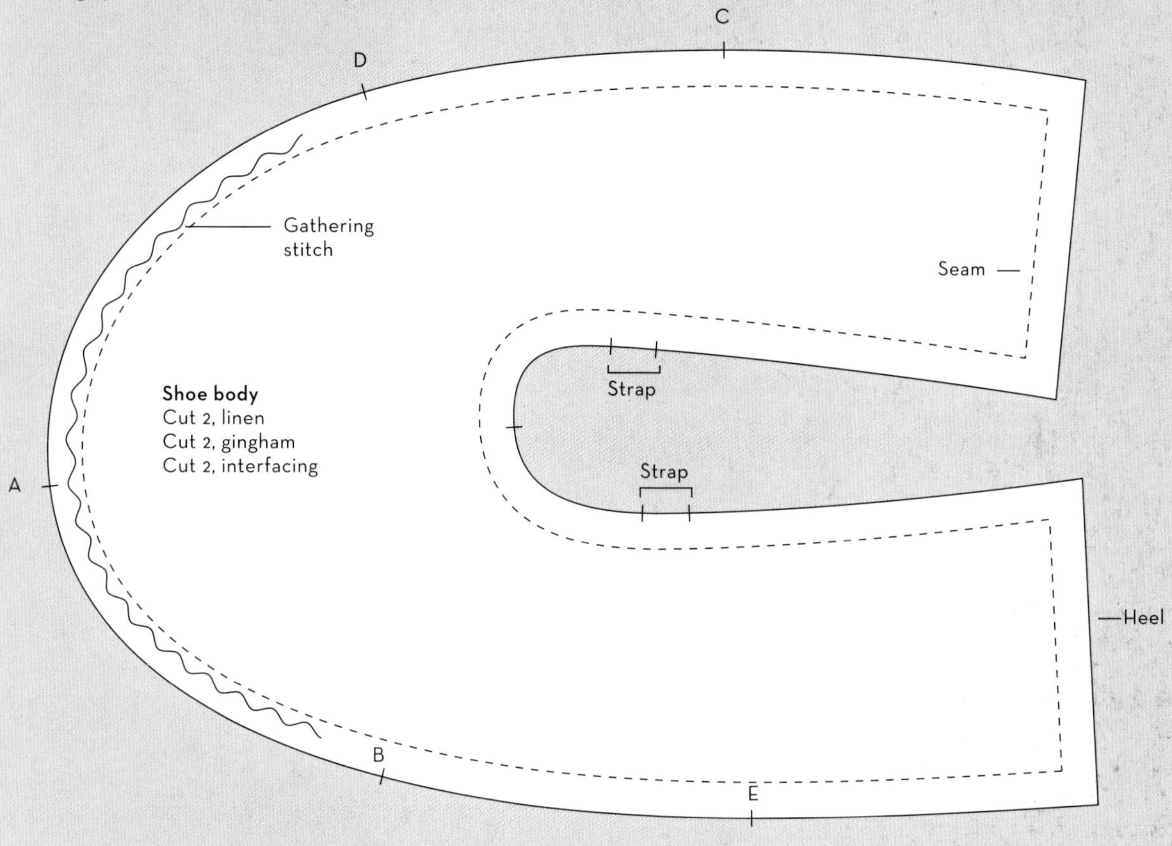

Gathering
stitch

D

C

Seam

Strap

Strap

Shoe body
Cut 2, linen
Cut 2, gingham
Cut 2, interfacing

A

Heel

B

E

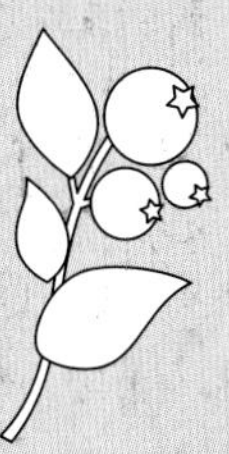

Blueberries
Template

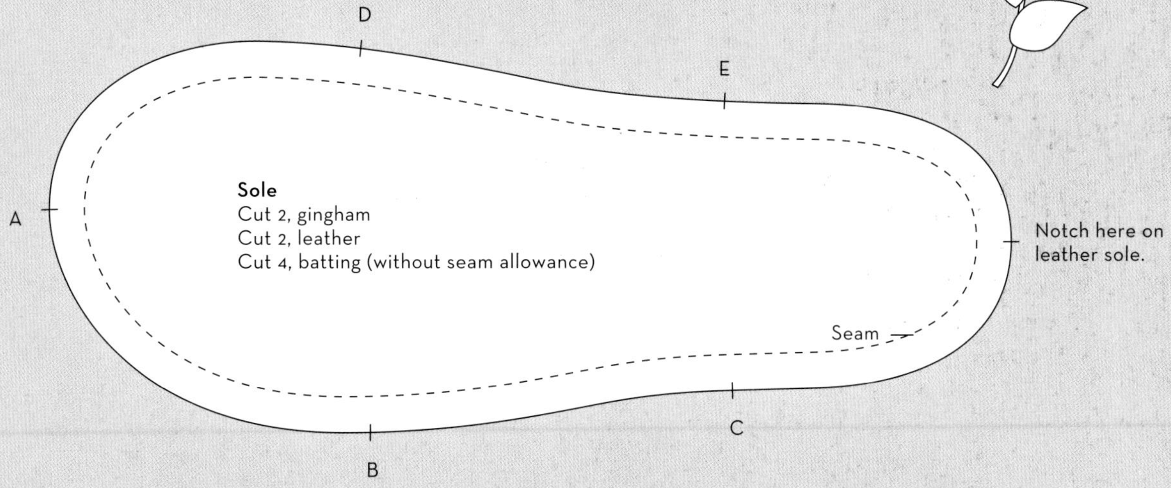

D

E

Sole
Cut 2, gingham
Cut 2, leather
Cut 4, batting (without seam allowance)

A

Notch here on
leather sole.

Seam

B

C

bird pillow

The bright splash of the colorful bird appliqué really stands out against the nubby brown linen on this pillow. This project makes a great accent for a homey living room or a child's bedroom.

Zakka Fact

Mixing and matching prints is very common in Japanese-designed zakka and can also be found in some of the fashions seen around the Harajuku neighborhood in Tokyo, which is known for its trendy, sometimes outlandish style.

Level of Difficulty

Finished Size

12" square

Materials

Scrap of brown linen, 29½" x 14"
   (for background)
Pink cotton, 11" x 9" (for bird)
Red striped cotton, 2 pieces,
   1¼" x 3" (for legs)
Yellow printed cotton, 3" square
   (for beak)
White-polka-dotted blue cotton,
   6" x 5½" (for flower)
Red-polka-dotted green cotton,
   ⅞" x 4" (for stem)
Embroidery floss in brown
   and white
All-purpose thread in red
   and brown
Embroidery needle
Bird Pillow pattern (see page 131)

Preparing the Fabric

CUT USING PATTERN
Pink cotton: 1 bird
Yellow printed cotton: 1 beak
Blue/white polka dot: 1 flower

Seam Allowance

1" seam allowance for pillow
   (pillow's French seams require
   large seam allowance)
¼" seam allowance for appliqués

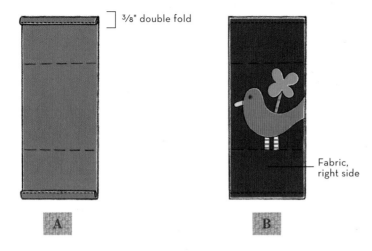

³⁄₈" double fold

A

Fabric, right side

B

1. Hem Edges

With the brown linen laid flat, fold up each short edge ³⁄₈" and press the folded edge. Fold each edge again ³⁄₈" in the same direction, and press the double fold flat. With brown all-purpose thread in your machine, edge-stitch (see page 10) each double-folded edge, backstitching (see page 11) at the beginning and end of your stitching (Drawing A).

2. Add Bird and Flower Appliqués

Prepare appliqués: Clip and notch the curves (see page 10) on each appliqué, making sure not to cut more than ¹⁄₈" into the seam allowance. With the appliqué fabrics wrong side up, turn each of the fabric's edges ¹⁄₄" to the wrong side, and press the edges flat.

Pin bird in place: Lay the bird body on the right side of the pillow front (see *Drawing B* for positioning). Note that the bottom of the bird's legs sit 8" from the bottom folded edge, and the end of the tail should align with the long raw edge of the fabric. Pin the bird in place using two or three pins in the center of the body. This will hold the bird in place but keep the edges free so that you can sew the other pieces before attaching the body.

Attach appliqués: Position the bird's beak and legs, and the flower stem on the pillow front, placing the edges of each appliqué under the bird, so the body overlaps each piece by about ¹⁄₄" *(Drawing B)*. Pin the appliqués in place.

With the red all-purpose thread in your machine, edge-stitch each appliqué, beginning with the legs and moving on to the stem and beak. Then edge-stitch the bird body, overlapping its edges over the legs, stem, and beak.

Place the flower overlapping the stem, and edge-stitch it to the pillow front.

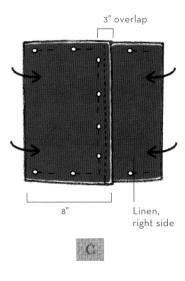

3" overlap

8"

Linen,
right side

C

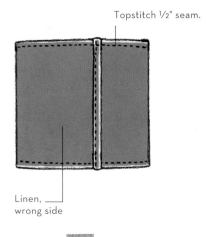

Topstitch ½" seam.

Linen,
wrong side

D

3. Sew Pillow Seams

The pillow seams are sewn with what's called a French seam, a very strong seam whose raw edges are neatly encased inside the seam itself. This involves sewing the edges being joined twice—once with the fabrics' wrong sides together and a second time with the fabrics' right sides together, as follows:

First, create the opening formed by the overlapping edges on the back of the pillow (through which to slip in or take out the pillow form). Lay the fabric flat, with the appliquéd right side facing down. Then fold each short end of the pillow 8" in toward the center so that the folded edges overlap by 3" *(Drawing C)* and pin the overlapped edges in place. Stitch the top and bottom edges together with a ½" seam (that is, stitch ½" from the raw edges), and trim the seam allowance to ¼".

Turn the pillow cover inside out so that the fabric's wrong side faces out. Topstitch the top and bottom edges again with a ½" seam, which will encase the raw edges *(Drawing D)*. Finally turn the pillow cover right side out, and press the cover and edges flat.

ZAKKA DESIGNER
kazu
http://www18.ocn.ne.jp/~fabric-k/

BIRD PILLOW PATTERN
(Enlarge patterns 200% on photocopier.)

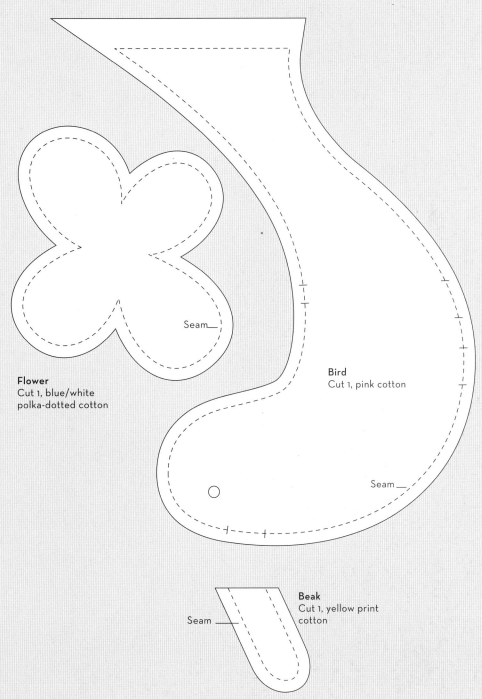

Flower
Cut 1, blue/white
polka-dotted cotton

Seam

Bird
Cut 1, pink cotton

Seam

Seam

Beak
Cut 1, yellow print
cotton

sashiko pouch

Here's a pretty little pouch
enlivened with sashiko stitching
to carry as a small bag, holding
lightweight items.

Level of Difficulty

Finished Size
10" x 9½"

Materials

Loose-weave turquoise cotton,
    2 pieces, 11" x 11¾"
Scraps of 5 different cottons
    for appliqués:
Fabric A: orange cotton, cut to
    circle, 5½" in diameter
Fabric B: cream-polka-dotted
    turquoise cotton, cut to circle,
    4¼" in diameter
Fabric C: cream cotton, cut to
    circle, 3¼" in diameter
Fabric D: purple cotton, cut to
    2¼" x 6"

Fabric E: cream-polka-dotted
    charcoal cotton, cut to 2¼" x 6"
Embroidery floss in cream, green,
    red, and purple
All-purpose thread in turquoise
Embroidery needle
50" length of ⅛"-wide braided
    rope, cut in half

Seam Allowance:
½"

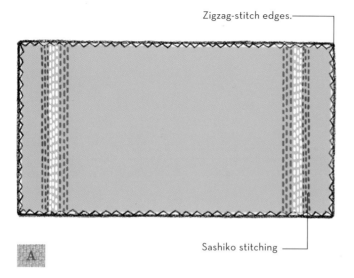

Zigzag-stitch edges.

Sashiko stitching

A

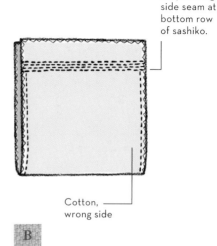

Stop sewing side seam at bottom row of sashiko.

Cotton, wrong side

B

1. Embroider Sashiko Stitches on Fabric

Before beginning the sashiko, set your sewing machine for a zigzag stitch and sew along all four edges of the turquoise cotton fabric to keep them from fraying.

Using the red embroidery floss in your embroidery needle and starting 1¼" from one short side, hand-sew three rows of sashiko stitching (see page 14), with each row ⅛" apart. Changing to the cream floss, sew three more rows, and finish with three rows using purple floss. The nine rows should be a total of 1" wide (*Drawing A*).

Repeat the process to add the same sashiko stitching to the fabric's other short side.

2. Sew Appliqués

Clip the curves of each appliqué circle and trim the corners of the appliqué rectangles by ⅛". Turn under the edges of each piece by ¼" and press the appliqués flat.

Pin the three concentric circles in place on one end of the fabric, with the largest on the bottom and smallest on top, referring to the photograph on page 133 and *Drawing F* on page 137 for the trio's placement. Embroider a sashiko running stitch around each circle, starting at the outer edge of the orange circle and working your way in. Use red floss on the orange circle and cream on the turquoise dotted circle, continuing the cream floss for the first three rows of the cream circle, and then switch to green floss for the remaining stitches that spiral into the center.

On the other side of the pouch, pin the first rectangle appliqué in place (see the photo on the facing page and *Drawing F* for placement) and attach it by embroidering 12 rows of sashiko stitching ⅛" apart with red floss. Pin the second rectangle over the first to make the cross, and attach it with 12 rows of sashiko stitches in cream floss.

Edge-stitch slit.

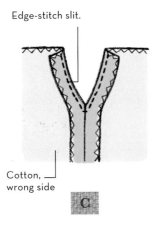

Cotton,
wrong side

C

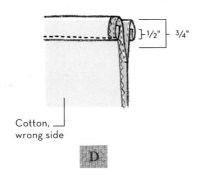

Cotton,
wrong side

D

½" 3/4"

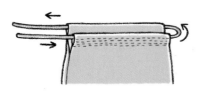

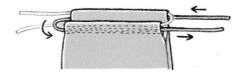

E

3. Sew Pouch Together

Fold the turquoise fabric in half with right sides together. Using all-purpose turquoise thread in your machine, sew both sides of the pouch, stopping at the bottom row of the sashiko embroidery *(Drawing B)*. Press the seams open.

With the pouch still wrong side out, edge-stitch (see page 10) the slit above the sashiko (see *Drawing C*) to finish off these edges.

4. Finish Top Edges

Turn and press each of the pouch's top edges ½" to the wrong side, then turn and press each edge again by ¾". Topstitch (see page 10) these double folds along the inner edge to make a tunnel through which you'll insert the drawstring *(Drawing D)*. Turn the pouch right side out.

To make the drawstring, insert one piece of the rope into the tunnel on one side of the pouch. Thread it through the tunnel to the other end, and back through the tunnel on the other side of the pouch, to where you began. Knot the rope's ends together. Repeat the process with the second piece of rope, starting on the tunnel on the opposite side *(Drawing E)*.

5. Finish Corners

Working on the pouch's right side, fold each bottom corner up by 1¾", and then machine-sew diagonally across the fold line *(Drawing F)*.

Attach the top of the folded corner triangle by sewing four short rows of sashiko embroidery across the corner, with purple floss which also adds a decorative element *(Drawing G)*.

ZAKKA DESIGNER
kazu
http://www18.ocn.ne.jp/~fabric-k/

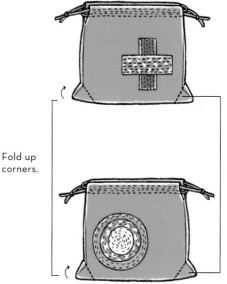

Fold up corners.

Machine-sew across fold line.

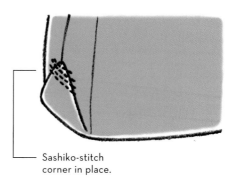

F

Sashiko-stitch corner in place.

G

handkerchief

White linen and sunshine colors
are a perfect combination for a
delicate handkerchief. Use
toweling fabric for this project
if you want to make a wash-
cloth, or turn a larger piece of
linen into a hand towel.

Zakka Fact

While linen handkerchiefs
are rarely seen in the
West these days, they're still
quite popular in Japan.
Women carry them daily
to use for drying their
hands in public restrooms,
which don't often stock
paper towels.

Level of Difficulty

- -

Finished Size

12" square

Materials

Scrap of white linen or cotton,
   12³⁄₄" square
Scrap of yellow felt, 4" square
Scrap of brown felt, 4" square
Perle cotton embroidery floss in
   yellow and grey
Regular cotton embroidery floss
   in brown
All-purpose thread in white
Embroidery needle

OPTIONAL: Double-sided fusible
   bonding product

NOTE: *For the handkerchief's
decorative circles, the designer
used iron-on felt, which is not
available in the U.S. at this time.
As an alternative, you can attach
regular felt to the handkerchief
with a bonding product designed
for fabrics that will be washed,
like Aleene's Platinum Bond Super
Fabric. Or you can just follow the
directions as given, and use
decorative embroidery to attach
the felt circles.*

1. Hem Edges

With the fabric laid flat, fold each of the four edges ¼" and press each fold flat. Fold each edge again, this time by ¾", and press and pin all the double folds.

Using the all-purpose white thread in your machine, sew the upper edge of the top and bottom double-folded hems, backstitching (see page 11) at the beginning and end of your stitching. Then similarly sew the two side hems. Sewing the hems separately will create nicely finished corners.

Using three strands of yellow floss laid along the machine stitching, couch (see page 12) the yellow floss with a single strand of grey floss in your embroidery needle.

2. Add Felt Appliqués

The handkerchief's felt shapes are purely decorative. Cut a few ovals, circles, and donut shapes from the yellow and brown felt to mimic those on the handkerchief (in the photograph opposite), or create your own shapes.

Attach the felt shapes to the hanky with a variety of embroidery stitches: Try a blanket stitch, running stitch, or whipstitch, (see pages 12, 14, and 15) around the cut shapes, using brown or grey floss on the yellow felt and yellow floss on the brown felt, or using a matching color of floss for a subtler look. Add a few French knots (see page 13) for decoration. Be playful with your design, but be sure to securely attach the felt appliqués to the fabric. To elegantly begin and finish your work, hide the beginning and ending knots in your floss by stitching into the underside of the appliqué.

ZAKKA DESIGNER
Miso Style
www.misostylejapan.com

squirrel
tea cozy

Animal tea cozies are cute!
This squirrel has so much
personality, and the thick felt
is great for keeping a teapot
warm. This cozy should fit most
one- to three-cup teapots.

Zakka Fact

The traditional tea
ceremony known as *Sado* is
integral to the culture
of Japan. In earlier times,
tea was a luxury only
available to noble families.
Learning the proper way to
serve tea is complicated
and being able to do it is
considered the mark of a
quite refined young woman.

Level of Difficulty

- -

Finished Size
exterior, 12" x 15";
interior space for teapot, 7½" x 9"

Materials
Thick grey wool felt, 15" x 24"
White embroidery floss
All-purpose grey sewing thread
Embroidery needle
Water-soluble disappearing-ink pen
Squirrel Tea Cozy pattern
   (see *facing page*)

- -

1. Make Front and Back
Cut two squirrels from the felt using the pattern, and use a disappearing-ink pen to transfer the sashiko stitching line for the tail to one side of both cut squirrels. Using three strands of white floss in your embroidery needle, embroider a sashiko running stitch (see page 14) with ⅛"-long stitches on both the squirrel front and back.

2. Sew Cozy Together
Align and pin the front and back of the squirrel, with wrong sides together. Then machine-stitch around the outer edge of the squirrel ⅛" from the edge (but *not* across the cozy's bottom edge), backstitching (see page 11) at the beginning and end of the seam. It's tea time!

ZAKKA DESIGNER
kabott
http://www.kabott.com

SQUIRREL TEA COZY PATTERN
(Enlarge pattern 200% on photocopier.)

— Seam

— Sashiko stitches

viking
key case

- - - - - - - - - - - - - - - -

Looking a little like a cartoon
Viking, this key case is big
enough to keep it in sight in
your purse but light enough
not to drag you down. The
Viking is made of ⅛"-thick
leather, but a nice thick wool
felt would work well too.

Zakka Fact

Scandinavian design is
adored in Japan today
and seen in everything
from textiles to home
accessories and furniture.
Hand-carved wooden
Viking figures probably
influenced this zakka
artist as she created this
clever piece.

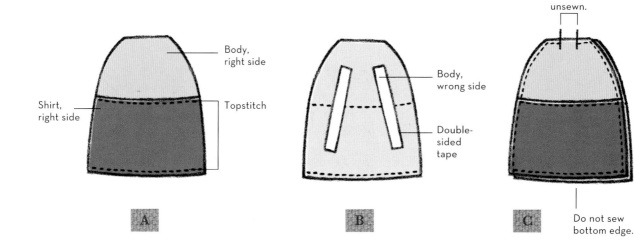

A

Body, right side

Shirt, right side

Topstitch

B

Body, wrong side

Double-sided tape

C

Leave ½" unsewn.

Do not sew bottom edge.

Level of Difficulty

- -

Finished Size

2¾" x 6½"

- -

Materials

Scrap of ⅛"-thick beige-pink
 leather, 7" x 4" (for body)
Scrap of ⅛"-thick brown leather,
 2¾" x 6½" (for shirt)
Scrap of ⅛"-thick orange leather,
 3" x 1½" (for helmet)
Scrap of ⅛"-thick beige leather,
 1" x 2" (for horns)
Scrap of ⅛"-thick yellow leather,
 1" square (for pocket)
Scrap of thin (¹⁄₁₆" thick or less)
 beige leather, 13" x ⅛"
 (for key-ring fob)
All-purpose sewing thread
 in cream

Heavy-duty machine needle
 (or regular machine needle if
 you're working with thick felt)
Metal key ring, ¾" in diameter
Acrylic paint in white, black,
 blue, and green
White glue
Double-sided tape
Viking Key Case pattern
 (see facing page)

- -

Preparing the Fabric

CUT USING PATTERN

Beige-pink leather: 2 bodies
 (transfer "stop stitching" marks
 to cut pieces)
Brown leather: 2 shirts
Orange leather: 2 helmets
Beige leather: 2 horns
 (cut 1 in reverse)
Yellow leather: 1 pocket

- -

Seam Allowance

None

1. Make Viking

Lightly glue one brown leather
shirt to the right side of one
body and edge-stitch (see page
10) the two together along the
top and bottom edges of the
shirt (*Drawing A*). Leave the sides
unsewn for now. Repeat the
process to attach the second
brown shirt to the second body.
Place two narrow strips of
double-sided tape on the wrong
side of each body piece, as
shown in *Drawing B*, and align
and press the two bodies, wrong
sides together, with your hands.
The tape will keep the pieces in
place as you sew them.

With the front and back bodies
taped wrong sides together,
edge-stitch them along both sides
and at the top, stopping at the
marks you transferred so that
you've left ½" of the top unsewn.
Do not sew the bottom edge
(*Drawing C*).

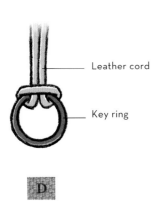

Leather cord

Key ring

D   E   F

2. Create Key Ring and Paint Face

Fold the thin leather strip in half, and attach its folded end to the key ring, as shown in *Drawing D*. Thread the other ends of the cord through the body from the bottom edge, so the raw ends emerge at the top of the body *(Drawing E)*.

Lightly glue the horns, right side up, to the wrong side of one helmet. Sandwich the top raw ends of the leather cord in between the front and back helmets and edge-stitch around the helmets *(Drawing F)*.

Paint the Viking's facial features with acrylic paint: green for the mouth, blue for the nose, and white with black dots for the eyes (refer to the photograph on page 147 for placing the eyes, nose, and mouth). Let the paint dry.

ZAKKA DESIGNER
pokožka
http://pokozka.web5.jp/

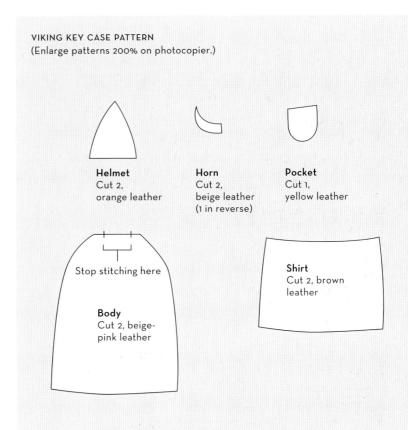

VIKING KEY CASE PATTERN
(Enlarge patterns 200% on photocopier.)

Helmet
Cut 2,
orange leather

Horn
Cut 2,
beige leather
(1 in reverse)

Pocket
Cut 1,
yellow leather

Stop stitching here

Body
Cut 2, beige-
pink leather

Shirt
Cut 2, brown
leather

SHOPPING FOR HANDMADE ZAKKA AND CRAFT SUPPLIES IN JAPAN

For zakka aficionados, a trip to Japan is a dream come true. The Nippori neighborhood in Tokyo has dozens of textile wholesale shops and is often called "Nippori Textile Town" or "Nippori Fabric Street." You'll also want to visit the Asakusabashi area, which is known for the many wholesale shops selling craft supplies, tools, dolls, toys, beads, silk flowers, and so on. The shops in both neighborhoods sell to the public, and the prices are quite reasonable. We've added some online shopping links below, but understand that most of these sources don't ship overseas. To get a better idea of their merchandise, you'll have to go to Tokyo!

Au Temps Jadis (Tokyo, Shibuya)
Offers a beautiful selection of lace, ribbons, buttons, and other trimmings from France, England, Italy, and Germany. You can enjoy their yummy crêpes at their café in the basement too: http://www.many.co.jp/jadis/.

Design Festa (Tokyo)
The biggest international art fair in Asia, with a huge section of handmade crafts. Held twice a year (May and November), it features both professionals and young crafters: www.designfesta.com.

Handmade markets (Kyoto)
There are several handmade markets held monthly. One of the bigger ones, held on the 15th of every month, is called Tezukuri Ichi (meaning "handmade market"), near the Chionji temple, and is an excellent source of handmade zakka and toys.

Kinka-do (Tokyo, Ikebukuro)
Another huge, crafty department store: http://www.kinkadou.com/shopInfo.php?shopId=1&brndId=8. The online store is: http://www.rakuten.co.jp/kinkado/.

Okadaya (Tokyo, Shinjyuku)
Department store that carries everything for sewing and some knitting supplies too: http://www.okadaya.co.jp/hobby/index.html. Their online shopping site, though just the tip of the iceberg, is: http://store.yahoo.co.jp/okadaya-ec.

Tokyu Hands (Tokyo)
DIY department store with several locations in Tokyo and floor after floor of fabrics, trim, tools, and craft supplies: www.tokyu-hands.co.jp. Their online store is: www.hands-net.jp.

Tomato (Tokyo, Nippori)
One of the most popular stores in Nippori Textile Town, they sell sewing tools, buttons, beads, ribbons, and more: http://www.nippori-tomato.com/tomato/2notion.html.

Yuzawaya (Tokyo, Kichijoji)
A crafter's heaven, much like Kinka-do and Okadaya but in a different neighborhood: http://www.yuzawaya.co.jp/. Their online store is: http://store.yahoo.co.jp/yuzawaya/index.html.

Glossary

Below is a small glossary of Japanese terms used in this book.

Amigurumi—Crocheted or knitted toys

Bento bag—Bag that many Japanese (especially girls) use to take their lunch to school

Bunko-bon—Small paperback book

Furoshiki—Japanese tradition of folding fabric to elegantly wrap packages or gifts

Karakusa—Pattern made up of scrolling leaves and vines

Kawaii—Cute, adorable

Konnichiwa—Hello

Koromo-gae—Seasonal change of clothing or zakka

O-uchi café style—"Home café style," a trend in which people decorate their homes with zakka cozies and other items used in the French bistros/cafés now prevalent in Japan

Sashiko—Traditional Japanese embroidery stitch

Take kago kinchaku bag—Drawstring bag with a bamboo bottom

Teruteru-bozu—"Sunshine boy" doll traditionally made by children to coax out the sunshine on a rainy day

Wagashi—Traditional Japanese sweets

Zakka—Term meaning "household goods," referring to beautifully designed, handmade goods like tea towels, coasters, and pillows

Resources

In case you are not able to find what you're looking for at your local craft store, here are some online resources.

CRAFT SUPPLIES

AC Moore
www.acmoore.com
(general craft supplies)

Ace Hardware
www.acehardware.com
(snap bolt clasp for House Camera Cozy on page 60)

Etsy
www.etsy.com
(wide range of all kinds of supplies, as well as a place to buy handmade everything)

Jo-Ann
www.joann.com
(fabric and general craft supplies)

Kitchen Emporium
www.kitchenemporium.com (brioche tins for Tartlet Pincushion on page 24)

Leather Craft Supplies
www.leather-crafts-supplies.com
(leather)

Michaels
www.michaels.com
(general craft supplies)

FABRIC AND NOTIONS

A Child's Dream Come True
www.achildsdream.com
(wool and hand-dyed felt)

Burnley and Trobridge
www.burnleyandtrowbridge.com
(period costume supplies, including nice linen)

Chadwick Heirlooms
www.chadwickheirlooms.com
(heirloom sewing supplies and linen)

eBay
www.ebay.com
(vintage linens)

Fabric.com
www.fabric.com
(wide variety of cottons and prints; some may require ½-yard minimum purchase)

Kari Me Away
www.karimeaway.com
(wool felt)

Kitty Craft
www.kitty-craft.com
(Japanese notions, fabrics, and books)

Linen Fabrics
www.LinenFabrics.com
(good selection of linens)

Linnet
www.lin-net.com
(store based in Kyoto selling wonderful Japanese fabrics and trim; ships overseas)

Magic Cabin
www.magiccabin.com
(wool felt)

M + J Trimming
www.mjtrim.com
(huge supply of trim and buttons)

PeriodFabric.com
www.periodfabric.com
(nice linen fabrics)

Purl Patchwork
www.purlsoho.com
(cute fabrics)

Reprodepot
www.reprodepot.com
(vintage, Japanese, and other fabrics; 1-yard minimum purchase)

Superbuzzy
www.superbuzzy.com
(Japanese fabrics, trim, and buttons; most fabrics require ½-yard minimum order)

Tinsel Trading
www.tinseltrading.com
(lovely trim, including ribbons and vintage trim)

Vogue Fabrics
www.voguefabricsstore.com
(wide variety of fabrics, including nice linens)

MISCELLANEOUS

Daiso
www.daiso-sangyo.co.jp/english
100-yen store (like a dollar store), selling lots of cute zakka; U.S. locations in Washington and California

Famima
www.famima-usa.com
(Japanese-style convenience stores)

Kinokuniya
www.kinokuniya.co.jp/english
(bookstores in New York, California, Oregon, and Washington known for their huge selection of Japanese craft books)

Mitsuwa Marketplace
www.mitsuwanj.com/en/index.htm
Japanese grocery, sweets, and specialty store, with locations in New Jersey, Illinois, and California

Takashimaya
www.takashimaya-ny.com
Large Japanese department store chain, with New York store at 693 Fifth Ave.: six floors of imported products

Crafting Japanese Blog
http://www.craftlog.org/craftingjapanese/ (bloggers review and comment in English on Japanese craft books and projects)

ACKNOWLEDGMENTS

We wish to thank all of the generous people who helped us along the way in creating this book, starting with the Japanese designers who contributed projects. Their handmade zakka inspired us, and we're excited to share their work with a wider audience. We would also like to thank Lilly Ghahremani for her advice and creative ideas and for getting the book placed with the perfect publisher. Beautiful zakka demands beautiful photos, and we're grateful to have had Yoko Inoue behind the camera, assisted by stylist Yuki Matsuo—their knowledge of and sensitivity to the zakka pieces surely helped make the photos stunning. Thanks also to Melanie Falick at STC, who shares our love for handmade things and helped turn an idea into a reality. And to technical editor Chris Timmons, the best in the business.

We would also like to thank all of our friends and family who supported us, with a special recognition of two people— Masanori Hase and Cal Patch—these angels were our secret weapon in getting the sewing techniques correct and the patterns perfect.

Thank you all!

Domo arigato!